Brother Bennie' book in regards to the challenge of South Asia is, in one word, unsurpassed! He carefully and systematically ushers us through the seven passages involved. I found it especially helpful to read chapter six in which he lists ten misconceptions concerning missions in general.

Dr. H. L. Willmington
Founder & Dean, Willmington School of the Bible
Founder & Dean, Liberty Home Bible Institute
Liberty University
Lynchburg, Virginia

"My friend Brother Bennie has given a great gift to the Christian church by writing "Passage to the Unreached." Where some books on world missions simply add to our load of guilt, Bennie helps us see and feel the difference one person can make whose heart is in tune with our mission-driven God. The incredible story of Alpha Ministries proves that with God, all things are possible. My hope is that this book ignites a movement that moves Christians everywhere to join the passage to the unreached for the glory of God."

Dr. Ray Pritchard
President, Keep Believing Ministries
Author: An Anchor for the Soul, Stealth Attack, Fire and Rain, The ABCs of Wisdom

"Brother Bennie, in Passage to the Unreached, has written a book that encourages all its readers to be involved in reaching people for Jesus Christ, by understanding the simplicity of missional work. Passage to the Unreached cuts straight to the heart of missions, which is the work of the local church. As you read this book you will see the biblical example and the great effectiveness of the local indigenous church in reaching its own people."

William Franklin (Will) Graham IV
Director of the Billy Graham Training Center at The Cove and Associate Evangelist of the Billy Graham Evangelistic Association

"Brother Bennie is a rare man. As I have observed him over the years, my trust in him has grown without pause. His integrity is real, not feigned, and his walk with God is so authentic that it inspires a sense that what he has found in Jesus Christ is worth laying down one's life for. There is a power and light about him that makes one want to know its source. Bennie is so mindful of being a good steward of the time God has given him, that the fact he has invested his time to write a book is assurance of it being necessary to read it."

Nathan Sanders
Sanco Homes Wilmington

"Alpha Ministries has proven to be faithful with the "Passage" God has called them to in the greatest unreached areas of the world. This has not been without tremendous hardships and sacrifices. Brother Bennie has written a God-inspired challenge concerning His purpose for the church. "Passage to the Unreached" will help clarify and magnify how God is using native preachers to reach the unreached. I have personally found Alpha Ministries to be faithful and frugal in their everyday operation. I do believe that is why God is giving them this great vision and harvest and why we have partnered with them for over twenty years."

Ben Manis
President
Reaching Souls International

"During 40 years of international ministry, I have traveled to five continents and worked with scores of churches and evangelical organizations. When I am asked to name the indigenous work to which I give my strongest commendation, I always name Alpha Ministry. This is a true New Testament ministry of evangelism, discipleship, and church planting. It was born out of sacrifice and faith, under the most difficult circumstances imaginable. Its growth has been supernatural, against all odds. Today, it is expanding throughout Asia and ultimately to be the most influential ministry in having an impact on North Korea for Christ.

My endorsement is not from one who has observed from a distance. I have been to the ministry's home ground in South Asia. I have participated in their training institutes. I have met and worked with the founder and his remarkable family. I have observed the dedication of their national evangelists. They are doing exactly what they say that they are doing, and more."

Dr. Wayne Bristow
Total Life International Ministries
Wayne Bristow Evangelistic Association

"Having been to the areas of the world where Bennie serves his Savior, I know the difficulties of doing ministry there. It takes a special breed, with a special calling and God's anointing, to be effective. When my wife and I first met Brother Bennie, and the following year his father, I could not believe the scope of their vision. I thought to myself, this can't be done by mortal man. Yet today, five decades later, the world is seeing the fulfillment of their vision.

Alpha Ministries started with nothing and has done without for so long that the only answer for what their ministry has accomplished, and is accomplishing, can be attributed only to the direct favor of God. This book, Passage to the Unreached, is a mere glimpse into the life of sold-out, selfless servants of Almighty God and an inspiring example of what you too can do to bring men to Jesus.

If you want to have your passion for the lost reignited, read this incredible account by Brother Bennie of sacrifice, faithfulness and victory."

Richard Headrick
President & CEO
The Headrick Companies

"What a Christian, what a ministry, what a need and what a book! Brother Bennie and Alpha Ministries are the face of missions today in this incredibly compelling book that tells the moving story of one of the purest ministries in the world that is devoted to reaching what will soon be the largest unsaved population on earth, the nation of India.

I have known the Mathews for many years, and know and have witnessed their sacrifices, commitment and integrity. I have taught in their conferences, preached in their crusades, trained their students and ordained their pastors. I know the struggles they have endured to fund their ministers and the incredible hardships they have faced. Yet, they have remained steadfast and believing in the face of such challenges. And God has honored them for it! I further have the privilege of calling Bennie a spiritual son and helping mentor this unbelievably humble servant of God. I highly recommend this ministry and this book to you. You will be moved and blessed. I promise that you will!

I have personally found Alpha Ministries to be faithful and frugal in their everyday operation. I do believe that is why God is giving them this great vision and harvest and why we have partnered with them for over twenty years."

Dr. Richard Heard
CT International Ministries

"I wish I had known of Brother Bennie much sooner in my ministry. From my first encounter with Bennie and his Mother and Father I was drawn to them and the Alpha Ministry. Bennie's wife and children demonstrate their love Jesus and their commitment to the Gospel.

In "Passage to the Unreached" you will be moved by their dedication to both love the Lord Jesus and live out their faith whatever the cost. It is not a book of guilt trips but a book of challenge and searching. Bennie's honest testimony to the saving life of Christ, often in a hostile environment, reads like the book of Acts.

My prayer is that many, as they read this book, will be challenged in their minds, moved in their emotions and committed in their wills to bloom where they are planted to reach their unreached with the Gospel of Jesus."

Ian Leitch
Evangelist and Bible teacher
The Heralds Trust, Scotland
Author: Life before Death

"I have known of Alpha Ministries since its beginning, because I have known Cherian Mathews for forty-eight years. Alpha Ministries has been and continues to be used of God in an incredible way. They are good stewards of God's provisions, responsible with sharing the Gospel, and have unquestionable integrity with the ministry God has given them."

Dr. Clyde Cain
Extension Coordinator, Shawnee Campus
SWBTS at Oklahoma Baptist University

My Dear Brother Cherian and Sister Grace:

"I have just read in "On Call" Alpha Ministries newsletter that you have reached the wonderful milestone of 45 years in ministry in your beloved India. I wish to congratulate you on your incredible faithfulness to the gospel under the most difficult circumstances. God has entrusted you with the most costly and therefore the most glorious mission this side of glory-the honor of suffering for His name-a ministry He entrusts to only a few, for few are willing to pay the price. Paul was writing to people like you when he penned Philippians 1:29, "For unto you it is given in the behalf of Christ, not only to believe in Him, but also to suffer for His sake."

"I thank you for permitting me to share just a little in your extraordinary ministry – with you and your three sons --Bennie, Finny, and Davis . . . We pledge to you our unceasing prayers, agape love, and all we can do to equip young servants of Jesus to share the glorious gospel with the lost masses of your beloved country and all Asia."

Bill Bennett
Mentoring Men for the Master

PASSAGE
TO THE
UNREACHED

Brother Bennie
with Dr. Daniel Reichard

For information about our mission write to:
Alpha Ministries
P.O. Box 444, Madison Heights, VA. 24572-0444
434-929-2500
www.AlphaMinistries.net

Interior & Cover design: Shannon Gaines

Library of Congress Copyright Office Cataloging-in-Publication Data
Title: Passage to the Unreached
Registration Number Txu1-765-340 © 2011
Alpha Ministries, P.O. Box 444, Madison Heights, VA. 24572

ISBN 978-0-99129-690-3

DEDICATION

To my father and mother, Pastor Cherian and Grace Mathews.

I thank the Lord for your lives and resolve to serve Him as a
living example for our family. You are my heroes and spiritual
champions. You inspired me to follow the Lord's direction
and remain obedient to His calling and purpose in my life.
Mother, your prayers always guided my path to follow Him.
Most importantly, I want to thank all the hard-working native
frontline missionaries in the 10/40 window.

ACKNOWLEDGEMENTS

It is common that those who read this section of a book are family or friends and folks who have contributed to this project. It is so difficult to list each and every one of you, and doing so I fear I might leave someone out. There are many people who have blessed my life.

My parents taught me to live by faith and look at things though God's eyes. They are the source of all the blessings in my life. Their lives are a living book for us to follow, and I thank my Lord for them.

While attending a conference in 1992, I heard a preacher say, "Behind every successful man there is a woman." After hearing that inspirational speech, I told my wife, "Perhaps I will have to quote that for you down the road." She said, "I don't want to be behind you, but beside you." Her answer inspired me. She said, "To be a successful person, you need a sound advisor." Down the road, the Lord taught me that I need Sound Advice, Sound Doctrine, Sound Principles, and a Sound Mind. Thank you, Lina, for being a wonderful life companion, mother, friend, confidant and burden sharer along life's journey. God has provided you to double my joy and divide my grief. Thanks also to my wonderful children Faith, Ben, and Joy. You are a gift from God and I love you.

I must say thanks to my brothers and sister Finny, Denny, Davis, Jimmy, and Lovely, and the rest of the family including every child in the Mathews clan who encourages me and in numerous ways, enables me to persevere in the task God has for me. Their excitement and confidence has compelled me to take challenges in life. I cannot forget Mr. P. J. Augustine, my father-in-love, who prayed me through this process, but went to be with the Lord on June 20, 2005. He desperately wanted to see this printed. In addition, thank you Mrs. Theresa Augustine, Pastor Wilson George, and family.

Thanks to my pastors and teachers. My father, Pastor Mathews Cherian, is the first preacher, teacher, and pastor in my life. Dr. Ezra N. Williams was my pastor from 1988 to 1994 while I was in New York City. He lit the fire in my heart for missions every Sunday until I became miserable and quit my man-made comfort zone and stepped out to serve Him. From 1996 until today, Pastor J. D. Surbaugh has been my pastor and teacher. He ordained me, and he has been a great teacher and mentor throughout these years. He reinforced God's Word to inscribe it upon my heart.

Mr. Bible, Dr. Harold Wilmington and Dr. Danny Lovett have influenced me academically. My dean, Dr. Wilmington, taught me how to study the Word and live by the Word. He is a godly example and inspiration. I will never forget how Dr. Lovett made me sweat in my Hermeneutics class. I did not like him putting me on the spot to preach. Thanks for the jumpstart. Dr. Vernon Brewer has a gifted mind and he is a gifted speaker. He saw what God made me to be and recognized the gifts and divine endowments God placed in me. Thank you for believing in and standing with me and helping me publish this book.

I owe a debt of appreciation and gratitude to all my friends and partners in ministry. A note of gratitude to Ben Manis, Dr. Bill Bennett, Pastor Butch Pursley, Pastor Carlton Brown, Dr. Chris Brammer, Dr. Clyde & Kay Cain, Clyde Minter, Dwight Holloway, Roy & Lowana Gallop, Frank Tettenburn, Pastor Frank Thomas, Jamall Badry, Dr. Jay Francis, Dr. Jerry Falwell Sr, Johnny Hall, Joyce & group, Mack Hounsel, Mark Saunders, Martin Fassero, Marty Sweat, Mike Rhodes, Nathan Sanders, Terry Carlson, Pastor Peter Ansah, Pastor Philip Dunn, Pitts Evans, Dr. Richard Heard, Richard Headrick, Steve Osburn, Dr. Wally Waldheim, Wade Taylor, Will Graham, Will J. &

Marie Roberts we treasure your friendship in the Lord. You are standing with us and witnessing what the Lord is doing.

I must say thank you to Dr. Dan Reichard Jr., my good friend and co-laborer for his suggestions and thought provoking insights. He displayed amazing patience as I worked out these written words verbally. I thank God for bringing him into my life. Thanks also to Eric Vess, my guru, who gave me practical and organizational wisdom. I must say thanks to number of friends who read the manuscript and made helpful comments. Daniel Bowden, Robin Anderson, Dana Williamson, Lovely, Koshy, Susan DeWalt and Faith Mathews.

And there are all of you—so many who pray for me regularly and encourage me in a multitude of ways. I thank my church family in Baroda, India and Madison Heights, Virginia who helped me along the way. There are far too many to mention here. Finally, a special word of thanks is directed to all unnamed others whose working, giving, and praying continue to make the native church planting movement a reality. I wish I could salute them all. Together, we give all the glory to the Lord of us all. To Him alone—our Jehovah-Jireh, our El Shaddai—be the glory forever. Shalom!

CONTENTS

Dedication
Acknowledgments
Forward
Introduction
Chapters:

Appendix: The Model Church

FOREWORD

It was the largest crowd I had ever spoken to in my life.

The last glimmers of sun faded as I looked out into a massive gathering of people. The colors of their clothes—yellows, oranges, and reds—were a brilliant sight.

I had never witnessed so many packed into one outdoor pavilion. More than 50,000 Hindu faces stared up at me, eyes intent and serious, as if searching for something they hadn't seen before.

I could sense they were desperate for something more than what the cycle of karma had been offering them for centuries. They were looking for hope—real hope.

For the next three nights, Brother Bennie and I were able to share the good news of the Gospel to tens of thousands of Hindus in the northern state of Gujarat, India. For most of them, it was the very first time they had heard the name of Jesus spoken.

I will never forget seeing hundreds walk toward the front of the stage to receive Christ. It was like seeing a river form out of a sea. The sounds of prayers being uttered aloud filled the air with an energy that was indescribable.

I exchanged looks of awe and disbelief with Bennie, who was smiling from ear to ear. He was witnessing his own people being freed from the bondage of reincarnation and works-based religion they had been enslaved to for their entire lives. Instead of searching for the shores of the Ganges River to wash away their sins, it was the blood of Jesus that was now making them new.

In that one surreal moment, I knew this is what Brother Bennie had been born to do.

Here in one of the most hostile places in the world for Christians, hope was springing up. Lives were being transformed before our eyes. The heaviness of a burden had been lifted, and God had used Bennie to do it.

Howard Thurman, an American clergyman and civil rights activist famously said, "Don't ask what the world needs. Ask what makes you come alive, and go do it. Because what the world needs is people who have come alive."

While many have dutifully responded to the last command of Jesus to share the Gospel with a dying world, few have grasped what it really means to "come alive." Too many have knowledge without passion. Too many are preaching and teaching about hope and joy that has never truly taken hold of them.

When I think of someone who has come alive because of Christ, I think of Bennie. I think of the impact he's making through Alpha Ministry's ever-expanding vision for the poor, the orphaned, and the unreached. His compassion, vision, and faith are truly remarkable.

Every now and then, but not too often, God raises up a man or woman that will make an incredible impact for His Kingdom. Bennie's partnership with World Help over the years has created countless opportunities to bring help and hope in places where it is scarce.

Every word of this book is coming from a man who has lived his life in such a way that is undeniably authentic and sincere. His encouragement to you and me comes from a legacy that continues to reach countless people throughout Asia and beyond.

Each page of Passage to the Unreached will take you on a global journey of discovery as you see the risks many have undertaken in pursuit of the Great Commission. You will be challenged to think about the unreached with more boldness and resolve than ever before.

I believe that God has a passage for all of us to follow, an adventure to live for His purposes. Don't waste any more time pursuing your own passages, however well- intended. I can say from experience that the only life worth living is one that is fully given over to God and the things that break His heart.

The passages Bennie describes in these pages brought me back to those three unforgettable nights in Gujarat, India. I know the experience was one of God's passages for Bennie and me—His version of a voyage that would ultimately change the course of so many lives, including our own . . . forever.

As you read these pages, it is my prayer that you will catch Bennie's vision. Just imagine what God could do with a life—your life—fully surrendered to His purposes.
The possibilities are limitless when you do.

Dr. Vernon Brewer
Founder and CEO of World Help

INTRODUCTION

Every time I think of the word "Passage", I envision an incredibly exciting adventure. I think of the men and women throughout history who have walked, sailed, and even flown into the unknown. Some of mankind's greatest achievements and discoveries came through courageous individuals casting off the ropes of safety and pushing out into a vast ocean of uncertainty.

John Leonard Dober and David Nitschman were two such men. In 1732, they stood on a dock and said their final goodbyes to family and friends. Some begged them not to board the ship, but it was too late to turn back. These two ordinary men had sold themselves into lifelong slavery. Their destination: the West Indies. There they would endure unbearable conditions for the sole purpose of sharing Christ with their unreached fellow slaves.

As their ship sailed away into the unknown, one of the men cried out, his voice carrying over the water, *"May the Lamb that was slain receive the reward of His suffering!"* Those words have echoed down through the ages and remain the call of Moravian missions to this day. These men were the first of the Moravian missionaries. Many of those who followed them packed their belongings in coffins, a testament to their resolve in the face of certain death.

John and David sold their lives for the Passage to the Unreached. God had called them and no logic or practicality would quench their passion. No thought of self would erode their purpose. They saw the Passage, they understood the consequences, and they acted.

THEY WERE NEVER HEARD FROM AGAIN.

Today, a Passage lies before us that is just as important as the passage to the West Indies. Other souls, equally precious to God hang in the balance at the other end. And we must travel through that Passage by partnering with native churches and using native church planters.

It may not be necessary to sell ourselves as to slaves, but we still must be slaves of God. We may not be called upon to leave our familiar soil, but we are all called to share the Gospel. We must each stand before an ocean of our own fear, put our trust in God, and push off, beginning our journey through the Passage to the Unreached.

Brother Bennie

The Passage
Chapter 1

> *"No one should fear to undertake any task in the name of our Saviour, if it is just and if the intention is purely for His holy service."*
> *- Christopher Columbus*

It is mysterious and legendary, great and intimidating. It has brought glory and failure, the fantasy of eternal youth, and the reality of death. It has been the hope of man even as it stretched through the darkness of the unknown.

IT IS "THE PASSAGE."

In 1492, Christopher Columbus made his historic voyage across the Atlantic. Columbus crossed the edges of his known world in search of a passage allowing Europeans to travel by water to the spice-rich subcontinent of India. While Columbus failed in his initial plan, he succeeded in discovering a passage that would take him, and countless generations to come, from the Eastern to the Western Hemisphere. Columbus failed to find spices in India, but he did discover the New World.

In 1513, Juan Ponce de León left his home in Spain and led an expedition through the brutally unforgiving region that is now the state of Florida. Today, Florida is one of the most frequented tourist spots in the world. But for Ponce de León, it was a mosquito-infested, snake-slithering, alligator-crawling swamp that left his men battling the local native Indians and diseases like malaria. He braved those dangers in search of the Fountain of Youth. He and his men believed that somewhere, hidden in those swamps, was a fountain whose healing waters could actually grant eternal life. Ponce de León was looking for the passage to immortality.

At the turn of the nineteenth century, President Thomas Jefferson commissioned Lewis and Clark to find a water passage from the eastern United States all the way to the unexplored western regions. Lewis and Clark accepted the challenge and set off through the great American wilderness. They didn't find the water passage they were searching for, but their efforts led to one of the first explorations of western North America. The knowledge gained by Lewis and Clark set the background and direction for all future exploration of a nation.

On July 20, 1969, Neil Armstrong stepped slowly from the lunar module *Eagle* and set his footprints on the surface of the moon. Amazingly, it had been only 66 short years since the Wright brothers had launched the first successful powered flight on the windswept shore of Kitty Hawk, North Carolina, by flying 120 feet in 12 seconds. What had challenged a nation to set its goals so high? Just as the Wright brothers had dreamed of a passage to the skies, our astronauts dreamed of a passage to the stars.

Today, there is a Passage that has eternal treasures and spiritual riches yet unclaimed, far surpassing anything that Columbus, Lewis and Clark, Ponce de León, or Neil Armstrong ever could have imagined. This Passage is both a doorway and a method to the unreached. It is the method of using native church planters to reach their own people

It is the endeavor of the church to reveal God to every lost man, woman, boy, and girl on this planet. It is the Passage that ultimately leads to the billions who have not heard the truth of Jesus Christ.

KEY ELEMENTS OF THE PASSAGE

Years ago my uncle, a new immigrant from India to New York City, bought a manual Volkswagen car for $500 at an auction. My uncle had never driven a car, automatic or manual. My aunt and others in my family were very upset at my uncle because he bought a stick shift car. Now he had to prove to them that he could learn. I was the only person in my family who had experience driving a stick shift, so the responsibility of teaching him fell on me.

On January 1, 1993, my uncle woke me up early in the morning so I could teach him to drive. I had come home late the night before because of a New Year's Eve service. To wake up on that freezing winter morning after only a little sleep was the last thing I wanted to do.

The month of January is one of the coldest winter months in New York. The car was covered in snow and when I got in, I realized the heater did not work. I was praying, "Lord, teach my uncle to drive today!" I didn't want to spend another morning like this.

I decided a large parking lot would be a good place to start. As we reached one, my uncle noticed there were small movements in some of the snow piles. He said, "Bennie, the snow is moving." I could not understand what he meant by "moving." But, as we drove closer to a big pile of snow, we saw white snow geese sitting in different pockets of the pile of snow. It wasn't the snow that was moving; it was the feathers of the birds ruffling in the wind.

As a new immigrant who was experiencing his first winter, my uncle said, "This is amazing Bennie, we are in this tin car with layers of clothing, but these birds are sitting on the ice without any coats or covers." He was fascinated. My uncle parked the car, got out, and walked towards the snow pile. The birds started to fly away.

Then my uncle said something interesting. "Bennie," he said, "Did you notice the birds fly away as I approached them? They are threatened by my presence because I am intimidating, and they do not know whether I am a friend or foe. They won't trust me enough to eat grains from my hand. You know why, Bennie? It's because they are afraid and unsure about our motives."

On many occasions, I have thought of his words spoken that cold winter morning. It is not only true with animals, but with people as well.

When Lewis and Clark searched for the Northwest Passage, they encountered many different Native Americans tribes and nations. Most of these Native Americans had never seen a white man before. They had no way of knowing if Lewis and Clark were going to befriend them or attack them.

Fortunately, Lewis and Clark had hired a French trapper and his Native American wife, Sacagawea. She gave directions to the expedition at critical moments. But, according to Lewis and Clark's own journals, her greatest asset was revealing to the Indians the explorer's peaceful intentions. Many times it was noted how her presence as a Native American woman opened the doors for cooperative interaction with the different tribes they encountered.

It is no different for us today. When western missionaries approach radically different cultures, the ones they are trying to help can feel threatened, distancing themselves and making progress very difficult.

In fact, this issue only seems to have worsened in recent years. The political climate is changing all around us. People are more suspicious the motives of others, and especially of foreigners. It is becoming very difficult for a Westerner to go and work in Asia on a long-term basis. Many of the countries are now closed to foreign missionaries.

Short-term missions, too, have inherent drawbacks. These mission trips are an exploding phenomenon in our culture. Almost every young Christian I know has gone, or plans to go, on a short-term missions trip to another country. While these can be life-changing adventures, the church can't solely rely on short-term missions to effectively impact unreached people groups for Christ.

I think my friend in India best summed up the mind-set of short-term missions. He said, "Bennie, when an American goes fishing, he wants to catch the fish. But many times he only wants his photo taken with the fish and then he puts it back in the water."

"Now when the rest of the world catches a fish, they take it home, clean it, cook it, and serve it to their family. Bennie, when you look at it that way, Westerners and the rest of the world fish differently. And it's the same with missions."

Historically, missions agencies have sponsored short-term missions trips so that people could 'experience' missions. In other words, they would go to another country, take some photos, sample the local food, learn a few of the native words, talk to people about Jesus, and then go home. It makes for a great 'National Geographic' experience, but it is a lot like the way Americans fish. They take the photo, go home, and tell the story. But the problem is, that kind of missions trip has no lasting effect on the people left behind in the field.

But the natives…the nationals…they have the vested interest. They not only have the compassion for the lost, they are also able to make a long-term impact.

So, if we are to reach successfully through the Passage to the Unreached, a key element must be using native, or national, trained workers . These are workers who look like those they are trying to reach for Christ. They talk like them, walk like them, dress like them, sit like them, and eat and drink like them. And while a Western missionary called and sustained by God can accomplish all God sets before him, I believe during this time in our history, using natives is the most effective use of our resources.

As we will see in the next chapter, this is a new wave of the modern missionary movement. It is the wave of native missions. It is like a brush fire fed by dry grasses before it and driven by the mighty winds behind it, consuming everything in its path. This fire is started and spread by winning nationals, training nationals, and sending nationals.

Dr. William Carey, the pioneer missionary to India, had envisioned this in 1800 when he said,

"It is only by means of native preachers that we can hope for the universal spread of the Gospel throughout the immense continent of India."

Throughout this book, the terms "native" and "national" are used interchangeably. The term "native" is used in its technical meaning, "Belonging to a particular place by birth." As an Indian, I refer to myself as a native of India and do not associate any pejorative meaning with the word.

A Brief History of the Modern Passage

Chapter 2

"I have but one passion - it is He, it is He alone. The world is the field and the field is the world; and henceforth that country shall be my home where I can be most used in winning souls for Christ.
- Count Zinzindorf

It was November 11, 1793. He could see the shoreline from the side of the boat. It had been a long and difficult five-month voyage at sea. As the distant landscape grew closer, the excitement grew in his chest as well. It had been years in the making, but William Carey was finally arriving in India. He had started out as a poor cobbler with a burden to take the Gospel across the world. His peers and advisors rejected his vision and told him not to go. He had already been turned back once, but finally he was here.

As Carey took his first steps in Calcutta he could not have imagined the hardships he would endure. He and his wife would lose two of their children to disease. His wife would suffer from delusions and paranoia, dying a few years later. Carey would become destitute, depressed, and almost lose his own life to disease.

Eventually, his faith and persistence was rewarded. Carey went on to establish a major church and develop a university. He translated the New Testament into 40 different languages and was the reason for the founding of the English Baptist Missionary Society. Millions of Christians in India owe their faith to Carey's efforts.

Christian missions did not begin with William Carey on the fateful day he stepped into India. But William Carey, and the movement he started, marked a new and exciting era of missionary commitment by the church. It was the dawn of modern missions.

THE WAVES OF MODERN MISSIONS

Missiologists have broken down modern missions into roughly 3 waves. Generally, it is held that the first wave began with William Carey in the late 1700s. The next wave of missions, known as "faith missions", was to more inland areas and began in the early 1850s with men such as Hudson Taylor. The third wave of missions began around 1935 by missionaries Cameron Townsend and Donald McGavran. These two men began to focus not so much on geographic areas as on isolated ethnographic people groups.

Alongside these "waves", other changes have marked different periods in modern missions. One of those differences was where the missionaries were coming from. First, they came from England, then later from America, and now they come from their own countries.

(1800-1900) "THE DAY OF THE ENGLISH MISSIONARY"

Missiologists call the 1800s, "The Great Century." During that time, many of those who followed in Carey's footsteps were from Scotland, Germany, Switzerland, Canada, and the United States.

Yet, it was a movement that began, and was primarily funded, by England and staffed by English missionaries. From the years of 1815 through 1891, England's Christian Missionary Society sent out more than 650 missionaries. Each of these men and women left family, friends, and security for foreign, unknown lands. But they did it to fulfill their calling to carry the Good News of Christ to those who had never heard that message before.

Adoniram Judson ministered in Burma for 37 years. During that time, he translated the Bible into Burmese and by the end of his life there were no fewer than 163 other missionaries helping him in Burma. Robert Morrison and Hudson Taylor served in China, each for 27 years. James Hepburn, Guido Verbeck, and Samuel Brown labored in Japan. In Korea, Horace Underwood and Henry Appenzeller served among the people. The South Sea Islands witnessed the missionary endeavors of John Paton, John Patterson, and John Geddie. Two of the better-known missionary adventurers, David Livingston and Robert Moffit lived and served on the "dark continent" of Africa. These men are just a few who toiled in "the Great Century."

During that same period, England had its ruling thumb over many countries. There was an expression the British people used with pride to describe their vast reach: "The sun never sets on the British Empire."

As the British spread their monarchy over other nations, its pride and greed grew as well. When trade became the principle factor for enlarging the Empire, they were blinded to any other purpose or vision, even to the point of restricting permission for evangelism and missionary work. They never truly stood for God or for God's people. From the story of William Carey, we understand how difficult it was for him to go and live in India. But it wasn't the Indian rulers who gave William Carey such a difficult time...it was the British government.

The British Empire owned many beautiful places in India as their vacation spots. Kashmir, Shimla, and the beaches of Goa became some of the most sought after destinations in the world. But as I stepped inside a historic British restaurant one day in Shimla, I came face to face with a sign that read, "Indians and Dogs Not Allowed." To the British, we were the same as dogs. The Indians were not deserving of the British God.

The Church of England never realized the Great Commission. They never understood the practical application of the biblical truth that all men were created equal. They never stood for God's Word or His mission to reach the uttermost parts of the world. Instead, they stood for the King and the Queen of England and for the proliferation of the British Empire at all costs.
Without a doubt though, the seeds that were sown and the labor that was invested by missionaries continue to reap a harvest even today. God is in control of every situation, and without His knowledge, nothing happens. He is the Alpha and Omega; He knows the beginning and the end. Paul speaks forth a valuable spiritual principle when he says,

> *"I have planted, Apollos watered;*
> *but God gave the increase."*
> *(I Cor. 3:6)*

A world of gratitude must be extended to these heroes of the faith and countless hundreds of others who spent their lives, and sometimes even gave their lives, so that the Gospel of Christ might go forth to all people. The harvest being reaped in the world today as part of the third wave is a direct result of what God did during the first and second waves of the modern missionary movement.

(1900-2000) "THE DAY OF THE AMERICAN MISSIONARY"

The 1900's saw the emergence of the United States as a leader in world missions. God raised the United States up as a powerful nation, built upon Judeo-Christian values and the grand experiment of democracy.

In spite of two world wars and a devastating depression, the work of missions marched forward. For me as an Indian, American Billy Graham, Dr. Bill Bright and George Verwer stand out for me as the most influential Christian evangelists of the 1900's. They invested their time, talents, and treasures not only to reach their homeland, but the nations as well.

DR. BILL BRIGHT AND CAMPUS CRUSADE FOR CHRIST

Dr. Bill Bright founded Campus Crusade for Christ. His desire was to reach not only students on campuses across America, but also to reach the nations through the "Jesus" film.

It is hard for Americans to understand the impact of the Jesus film in other countries. When the film came to India, the only television channel was the national channel. To receive that one channel, people had to pay to hook up their televisions to a big antenna, and the hook-up only worked from 6 p.m. to 11 p.m. It was a short 5 hours of government broadcasting. In contrast, the majority of the cities had big, air-conditioned movie theaters. It was a treat for people to see moving images and talking people on a screen. There was a big hunger for movies. It was during that time, in the early 1980s and '90s, that Alpha Ministries was able to reach tens of thousands of Indians with the Jesus film.

In the villages, we used a very effective strategy to show the film. During prominent religious holidays and festivals, every block and neighborhood would collect enough money to install a god or goddess related to that particular festival. Specifically, the Ganpati festival has always been celebrated elaborately in the states of Gujarat and Maharashtra. It is the great Hindu festival of Ganesh, the elephant-headed god of wisdom and prosperity. In each community, a tent was raised and a statue of Ganesh installed. After a ten-day time of pooja (prayer) and celebration, people would carry the statue in a procession of dance and mantras, eventually immersing it into a body of water. Hindus believe that Ganesh will take their misfortunes with him.

Funds are needed for these tents to be raised by each community. In those days, if any money was left over, it would go to rent a projector and screen so the community could watch movies. Youth would go door to door and collect money from people saying, "If you give a big donation, then we can install a big idol in our neighborhood and the gods and goddesses will shower blessings onto our community." Along with the religious benefits, the neighborhood could enjoy a night of family fun. Young children would insist that their parents give more money so that they could watch a free movie.

During these times, when televisions were rare and movie watching was a privilege, our missionaries would go to a community and tell people about a free big screen movie. They were curious to watch a movie about a God called Jesus, and best of all they didn't have to pay any money to rent a movie projector or screen. All they had to do was get their friends and relatives together by 8 p.m.

The vision of Dr. Bill Bright, realized through Campus Crusade for Christ and the Jesus Film Project, changed India forever. Jesus became God in human form to those who were worshipping idols dreamed from wild imaginations. We have seen and personally experienced the tremendous results. It has been instrumental in reaching thousands upon thousands with the Gospel around Asia.

George Verwer and Operation Mobilization

Born and raised in New Jersey, George Verwer is a man who has greatly impacted Asia and the world through his organization, Operation Mobilisation. He is also known for wearing his trademark bomber style jacket with a globe printed on the back, leading to his nickname, "bomber jacket man."

I had the opportunity to meet George at Billy Graham's Amsterdam 2000 conference. He passionately carried an inflatable globe to all the missions meetings. When I saw that, I thought of the phrase, "Been there. Done that. Got the T-shirt." George has been to so many unreached countries across the globe, reaching out to a lost world and meeting their needs. He has proved, time and time again, the reality of his love for those who still need to hear the message of Jesus Christ.

At a very young age he became involved in raising money for missions, focusing on Bible distribution. It all began when Dorothea Clapp began to pray faithfully for the students in her high school, asking God to touch the world through the lives of the young people she taught. Dorothea gave a copy of the Gospel of John to one of her students, George. He had been making quite a stir so she put his name on the "Holy Ghost hit list" and prayed, "Lord, make him a missionary."

On March 5, 1955, when Billy Graham came to preach at Madison Square Garden in New York City, someone persuaded George to attend and gave him a free seat on the bus. That night, transformation and salvation through Christ became a reality in his life. Back at school, he received permission to give out the Gospel of John on campus and 1,000 students made a commitment to read it.

George enrolled in college and then transferred to the Moody

Bible Institute. Ron Wilson, a man who spent many years as an entrepreneurial editor and the leader of the Evangelical Press Association, remembers that George Verwer, as a student, would come into its bookstore and pull the evangelistic tracts that had been damaged and discarded out of the trash. "No doubt," Ron said, "he went into Chicago's streets and passed them out."

Coming back home for Christmas, he organized a Christmas event at the high school auditorium. About 600 people came to that meeting and 125 stood up and trusted Christ. One of them was George's father. That high school just outside of New York City in New Jersey was the birthplace of Operation Mobilisation (OM).

Passion for the unreached gripped George's heart and made him a mission's mobilizer. His passion was contagious and he used it to involve others to do what virtually no other Americans were doing at the time; accomplishing missions through the use of nationals. As he began to share his vision, hundreds of Christians responded. Soon, about one hundred thousand men and women went with OM on missions. Some went for a summer and some for a year. An amazing number are still involved in missions in different ways.

OM has always sought to partner with a nation's local churches as part of their mission's vision. I remember OM teams coming to my family's town and village in India. These teams came frequently and helped my parent's ministry and the ongoing outreach work. It was an uncommon thing to see a team of young men and women from India working together with a group of westerners. These dedicated men and women came with a passion for Christ and a willingness to suffer for His name.

They gave their lives to His service and went without the

conveniences normal western missionaries enjoyed. The OM teams lived in our homes and ate and drank with us. They stayed in our churches with their sleeping bags and helped in outreaches. They were willing to come along side our native Indian missionaries and help in church planting work.

Their work came at a critical time. In the early 1970s, unlike today, westerners were welcomed in Asia and it was much safer for them to travel and live in villages. People did not know the word "terrorism" and were not indoctrinated with hatred for the West. They did face persecution, but the government still allowed them to work openly. Today, that freedom does not exist and many people in India only view Christianity as a western white man's religion.

At a time in India when television and other media outlets didn't exist, people read more. George Verwer's Operation Mobilisation teams provided Bibles and other Christian literature, and then helped our native evangelistic missions and missionary workers with the distribution.

The scope of Operation Mobilisation has grown over the years. They have three ships, the Doulos, Logos2, and Logos Hope, that have served the nations since 1970. These vessels have visited 140 countries and reached out to over 30 million people. On shore, approximately 100 million have been reached through this ministry.

George Verwer and OM international have left a lasting impact on world missions in Asia and Europe. They showed us that there is value in getting people out of their countries to help others face to face. Those receiving the teams as well as those going out were equally blessed. It has proved to be a vital part of God's harvest in both evangelism and church planting.

George once said, "As we inform ourselves about missions we

need also to sense the weight of responsibility to take action. It is possible to even be a missionary and yet not really take ownership of the bigger vision and task. Taking ownership means prayerfully developing goals and aims." We have seen George Verwer demonstrate that through his life and ministry. I remember as a young man how excited our national grassroots evangelists and pastors were when Billy Graham and the BGEA (Billy Graham Evangelistic Society) organized its first 1983 International Congress of Itinerant Evangelists, held in Amsterdam.

DR. BILLY GRAHAM AND THE RISE OF ALPHA MINISTRIES

Dr. Billy Graham had participated in, and led, many similar conferences in the past. The first was with a Youth for Christ function held in Beatenberg, Switzerland, in 1948. The purpose was to discuss more effective ways to reach the whole world with the Gospel. In 1966, in conjunction with Christianity Today, Dr. Graham helped organize and fund the Berlin Congress. Out of this meeting came a new trust among leaders across a broad spectrum of the Christian world. The BGEA sponsored a major conference in Lausanne, Switzerland, in 1974, to grapple with principles, concepts, methods, tools, and strategies to reach the whole world in the modern generation. The Lausanne Covenant continues to be a helpful guideline for ministries everywhere.

In 1983, 1986, and 2000, the BGEA held meetings in Amsterdam for Christian workers particularly involved in evangelism. The first two meetings were called the International Congress of Itinerant Evangelists (ICIE) 1983 and 1986, respectively. The third event was called Amsterdam 2000.

In 1983 India, modernization and globalization were not on the agenda when an evangelist or missionary couldn't even afford to buy a local bus ticket to go and preach in another village. Most of our national evangelists didn't even own bicycles. They had to walk from village to village.

Flying on a plane was only a dream. While visiting Bombay, it was a special treat to go to the Santa Cruz Airport and see the planes landing and taking off. I could not even think of a time when I might be lucky enough to actually take a flight.

An Indian could never afford to attend any of the ICIEs. But, the conferences were completely sponsored by the Billy Graham Evangelistic Association; they paid the airfare and lodging of all the participants. This 10-day conference was "by invitation only" with delegates who were evangelists from around the world, 75 percent of whom were from emerging nations.

This was the opportunity of a lifetime for many of our frontline evangelists, preachers, and leaders in India. They were amazed that someone had thought of them. BGEA saw to it that during these times, ordinary men and women, who never came on the radar of the elite in India or in other countries, were treated with a special opportunity to rest, retreat, and receive from God.

Indian evangelists had been praying the prayer of Jabez found in Chronicles, asking God to "expand [their] borders" so they could reach more men and women for Christ. Soon, the Spirit of God helped them experience that reality. A trip to Amsterdam proved that God was increasing the reach and influence of Christians in India.

I remember when the team representing Alpha Ministries, including my mother Grace, attended the Amsterdam '86 Conference. Dr. Graham looked at the hundreds of missionaries and church leaders and graciously rebuked them. He called them to accountability for failing to develop national leadership. He challenged the nationals to go back and start movements to contextualize the task of discipling the nations, and to develop national leadership to take responsibility for the

Great Commission. The challenge before us was to change the methodology and call on national churches and movements to take on indigenous forms and methods to communicate the Gospel.

Our team returned to India with a desire to raise awareness and initiate the church planting movement. Alpha Ministries began to teach and implement the changes the conference addressed. Conference attendees were given time to teach in our churches. Their experience inspired Christians in India and challenged them to grasp a new vision from God.

Following Amsterdam, my father organized the first pastor's conference in Baroda, India. Those who attended his conference took upon their hearts a new vision to develop leaders in their local churches. This conference continued yearly with 20 to 50 leaders and regional pastors attending each year. The numbers of attendees rapidly increased. We were overwhelmed with the number of pastors and leaders who desired to experience this type of retreat and training.

As time went on, the Alpha Ministries family continued to grow, but there were requests by church leaders from all over North India to spend time with my father and learn his vision. It was out of that hunger and the training at Amsterdam that Alpha Ministries organized our first large scale IMPACT (Indian Missionaries & Pastors Access Cross-cultural Training) conference in 1990.

My father believed that such an Alpha IMPACT Church Planters Conference would be a blessing to the native leaders of North India. But how could he sponsor such a large and expensive undertaking? Not only was I the oldest son, I was also the only son holding a job. I was working in New York at a hospital and studying to become a medical terminologist. Not feeling specifically led to the full-time ministry, I was attempting to make "millions for God" in the United States. But, the more

God spoke to my father about the conference and the more I saw the value of it, I sensed God would use me to be a part of the solution.

I began to work two full time jobs. During the day, I worked at a hospital in White Plains, New York, and at night in Bronx, New York, at Lady of Mercy Hospital. The income from the first job would cover my family's living expenses in New York, and the income from the second would be given, in its entirety, to Alpha Ministries for the cost of the conference. I believed in what my father was envisioning. I also believed in the cause to train and equip frontline leaders.

The conference was not an easy undertaking. It took a lot of prayer and planning to take that giant step. Over 300 pastors and leaders were invited from all over North India. The vision and desire was to teach, strategize, and initiate the church planting movement. Each pastor and leader who attended agreed to train two others and plant two new house churches within the next two years.

Since that first conference, Alpha Ministries' adaptation of BGEA's training strategy has produced more than 26,000 alumni scattered all over North India, Nepal, and many other countries of Southeast Asia and Africa. With God's help, we were able to pass on what we learned from our missionary predecessors. We were able to create a training package that was culturally relevant to our people in India and Southeast Asia.

An estimated 30,000 house churches have started as a result of IMPACT training. That training continues to be one of the most anticipated events in North India. Held every fall, it brings not only the Alpha church planters and leaders together for a week of Bible teaching, preaching, and worship, but also brings leaders from other evangelical groups in North India. These are native leaders. While some American and other Asian church leaders may have a part in the conference as invited speakers, it is and always has been a native led movement.

My brother Finny and I had the privilege of attending Amsterdam 2000. We heard Dr. Billy Graham say, "In the midst of the rapid change in almost every phase of our lives, the task of worldwide evangelization remains a priority of the Body of Christ. Decay in the societies of the world, consternation in the governments, and a deep heart-cry for revival throughout the Church of our Lord Jesus Christ all point to the need of the Savior in our world. The Lord of the harvest has many servants who are doing extraordinary work in bringing the Gospel to those who still sit in darkness. Their stories need to be known, their strategies multiplied, their commitments deepened, and their fellowship enriched within the body of Christ."

MODERN MISSIONARY MOVEMENT (2000 - PRESENT)

"The Day of the Native Missionary"

The vision of William Carey, now expanded to worldwide proportions, is becoming a reality: "It is only by means of native preachers that we can hope for the universal spread of the Gospel." This is the new wave of modern missions. It is a period of time when the native missionary and church are emerging as the major on-site messenger for evangelization and church planting in the world.

This new wave is simply a continuation of what God has been doing in the preceding waves. It is the miracle of God's Word doing what God's Word will do. It cannot be humanly explained. It is the Holy Spirit of the Living God taking His Word into the entire world. Here are just a few illustrations of what God is doing to reveal Himself to the nations of the world:

- A translation of the New Testament is begun in a new language every 14 days. At the rate in which Bible translations are being completed, at least some portion of the Bible will be translated into every language by the year 2020.
- In China, a land where foreign missionaries are not allowed and the public practice of Christianity is prohibited, it is estimated that there are at least 80 million believers. Some even estimate that the number may be as great as 100 million. Over 30,000 Chinese come to know Christ every day.

- In the late 1980s, it was estimated that there were 70,000 people being saved each day. Today, just 20 short years later, there are almost 180,000 people being saved every day. Worldwide, 3,500 new churches open each week.

- Over the last ten years, the number of new Christians in the world has grown by 300 million. Of these, about 10 million are from North America and Europe and the rest, 290 million, are from developing countries like Africa, South America, India, and China.

- More than 36 percent of the population of Russia, about 100 million, now profess to be born again Christians.

- One hundred years ago there were no evangelical churches in Brazil. Today, there are over 100,000 evangelical churches and an evangelical population of more than 50 million believers.

- South Korea is one of the most prosperous countries in the world today. There are 2,000 churches in Seoul alone. In South Korea, almost one-third of the entire population profess to be "born again" Christians. Three of the largest churches in the world are in South Korea, some with memberships exceeding 800,000. The vast majority of these Koreans have come to know Christ in the last 50 years, almost entirely through the efforts of native church leadership.

God is doing a tremendous work, and we are privileged to see it and be a part of it. It is not simply a fluke or an interesting trend. It is a mighty moving of God across the entire earth. It is more powerful than a tidal wave and no man-made border can stop it. No dictatorial principality can dissuade it, no language barrier can withstand it, and no religion can deny it. It is God revealing Himself to the world He created and for whom He died. Now, it is time to shout that message with a voice as loud as God's as we reach out to the unreached.

"Almost every page of the Gospel of John speaks of mission as sending, with regard to Jesus and with regard to us as well. Jesus did not come on His own, but His Father sent Him (John 8:42). He did not speak His own words but the words of the Father who sent Him (3:34; 7:16; 12:49). He did not do His own works but the works of the Father who sent Him (5:36; 9:4). These works were His miracles. He did not come to do His own will but the will of His Father who sent Him (5:30; 6:38). Like Jesus, we must receive a supernatural message, a supernatural ministry and a supernatural motivation to enable us to fulfill our mission."
-Paul R. Orjala

"Not called!" did you say? "Not heard the call," I think you should say. Put your ear down to the Bible, and hear Him bid you go and pull sinners out of the fire of sin. Put your ear down to the burdened, agonized heart of humanity, and listen to its pitiful wail for help. Go stand by the gates of hell, and hear the damned entreat you to go to their father's house and bid their brothers and sisters and servants and masters not to come there. Then look Christ in the face - whose mercy you have professed to obey - and tell Him whether you will join heart and soul and body and circumstances in the march to publish His mercy to the world."
-William Booth

GOD IS A GOD OF MISSIONS. HE WILLS MISSIONS. HE COMMANDS MISSIONS. HE DEMANDS MISSIONS...

*"Let the heavens rejoice, let the earth be glad; let them say among the nations, "The LORD reigns!"-1 **Chronicles 16:31***

*"Sing to the LORD, all the earth; proclaim his salvation day after day. Declare his glory among the nations, his marvelous deeds among all peoples."-1 **Chronicles 16:23-24***

*"My house will be called a house of prayer for all nations." -**Isaiah 56:7***

*"Sing praises to the LORD, enthroned in Zion; proclaim among the nations what he has done." -**Psalm 9:11***

*"All the ends of the earth will remember and turn to the LORD, and all the families of the nations will bow down before him, for dominion belongs to the LORD and he rules over the nations." -**Psalm 22:27-28***

*Again Jesus said, "Peace be with you! As the Father has sent me, I am sending you." -**John 20:21***

*"How, then, can they call on the one they have not believed in? And how can they believe in the one of whom they have not heard? And how can they hear without someone preaching to them? And how can they preach unless they are sent? As it is written, "How beautiful are the feet of those who bring good news!"-**Romans 10:14-15***

*"The Lord is not slow in keeping his promise, as some understand slowness. He is patient with you, not wanting anyone to perish, but everyone to come to repentance." -**2 Peter 3:9***

*"He that winneth souls is wise." If any man, women, or child by a godly life and example can win one soul to God, his life will not have been a failure. He will have outshone all the mighty men of his day, because he will have set a stream in motion that will flow on and on forever and ever." -**Dwight L. Moody***

The Challenge of the Passage

Chapter 3

"In the vast plain to the north I have sometimes seen, in the morning sun, the smoke of a thousand villages where no missionary has ever been."
- Robert Moffat

During one of my visits back to India, the only option for traveling was by bullock-cart, a two wheeled cart pulled by oxen. A small man with a turban and long mustache used his hands and feet to control the two large oxen that were pulling the cart. The oxen were obedient in response. To slow the oxen, he would press his feet between their back legs, and they would slow down or stop. To accelerate, he would twist the tails of the oxen, and they would start running. It was impressive to see a slight, 95 pound man control two oxen, each weighing over 900 pounds.

To start a conversation I asked the man, "Do you know that someone controls the world as you control the oxen?" He said "Maybe, who knows?" I asked him, "Do you know about Jesus?" He paused and replied, "Which village does he live in?" I told him, "I am not talking about a man but about a Savior, God." He replied, "No sir, I have never heard about that person."

We go into many villages in India and ask someone, "Do you know Jesus Christ?" The response too often is, "No. I do not. I do not believe that anyone by that name lives in this village." That is the tragic truth. They have not even heard Jesus' name.

The Passage represents a very real challenge. Millions upon millions of souls are at stake and God has chosen to use us to help Him reconcile these people to Himself.

We must begin by understanding and confessing that we can do nothing apart from God. We must seek His face, pray for the unreached, and be willing to serve in whatever capacity He chooses. We must also understand the challenges of the Passage so we can pray intelligently, invest wisely, and strategize effectively.

First, let's be very clear about who we mean when we say "unreached". The unreached, in the strictest sense, would be anyone who has never had an opportunity to hear and respond to the Gospel of Jesus Christ…people like the man who drove the bullock-cart. The "unsaved" are different from the unreached. The unsaved are those who, regardless of how many times and how clearly they have heard the Gospel of Jesus Christ, have not repented from their sins and accepted Jesus Christ. Thus, all unreached are unsaved, but not all unsaved are unreached. The greatest concentration of unreached people fall into an area commonly referred to as the 10/40 window.

WHAT IS THE 10/40 WINDOW?

The 10/40 window has become a popular name to refer to a rectangular area that extends from West Africa to East Asia. Its range is from 10 degrees north to 40 degrees north of the equator.

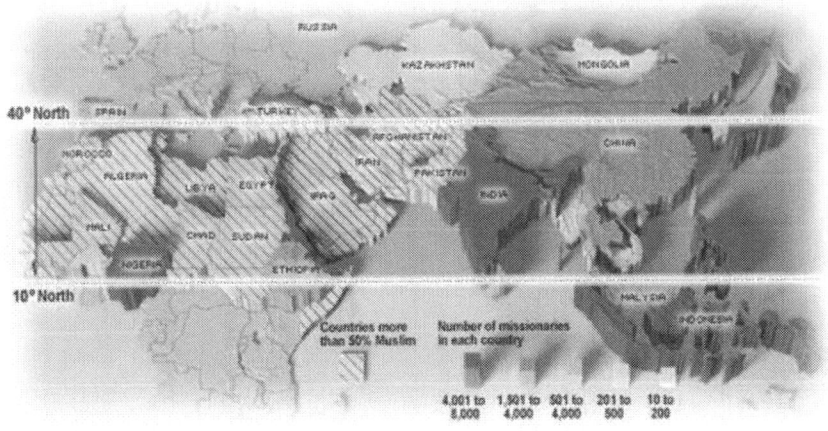

WHAT COUNTRIES ARE INCLUDED IN THE 10/40 WINDOW?

Roughly 59 countries that make up the 10/40 window. Some of them are:

Afghanistan, Egypt, Japan, Morocco, Syria, Algeria, Eritrea, Jordan, Myanmar (Burma), Taiwan, Bahrain, Ethiopia, North Korea, North Tajikistan, Tunisia, Bangladesh, Gambia, Thailand, Turkey, Benin, Gibraltar, Nepal, Niger, Turkmenistan, Bhutan, Greece, Kuwait, Oman, United Arab Emirates, Burkina Faso, Guinea, Laos, Pakistan, Vietnam, Cambodia, Guinea-Bissau, Lebanon, Philippines, Foreign Sahara, Chad, India, Libya, Portugal, China, Iran, Macau, Qatar, Cyprus, Iraq, Mali, Saudi Arabia, Djibouti, Israel, Malta, and Senegal.

- Of the seven billion people who live in the world today, four billion live in this relatively small, "window-shaped" area.

- Ninety-seven percent of all people living in the least reached countries live in the 10/40 window.

• It is estimated that there are about 10,000 unreached people groups in the world today. Of those, about 60 percent are closed to North American missionaries.

• Each day, an average of 50,000 people from the 10/40 window will die and slip into eternity without ever hearing a clear presentation of the Gospel.

WHAT RELIGIONS DO INHABITANTS OF THE WINDOW PRACTICE?

The 10/40 window is the birthplace of the world's most ancient religions; Judaism, Christianity, Islam, Hinduism, and Buddhism. The vast majority of the 2.1 billion people who make up the window adhere to Islam, Hinduism, and Buddhism. These people are born into countries that often outlaw, or at the very least, strongly discourage the practice of any religion other than the one the state endorses. They marry spouses of the same religion and raise their children just as they were raised, to be faithful to their gods. Their religions are an inseparable part of their life and worldview.

Each of these religions is complex and with the exception of Islam has views that may vary widely. But here are some of the basic, and much abbreviated, beliefs of each:

BUDDHISM

It is estimated that approximately six percent of the world's population are adherents of Buddhism. Founded by Siddhartha Gautama (Buddha) in India during the sixth century B.C., Buddha was searching for an answer to the questions, "Why is there suffering in the world? Why is there a class system in Hinduism?" His search led him to be "enlightened." Thus he became "The Enlightened One," or, "The Buddha." He surmised that there are "Four Noble Truths."

These truths are as follows:

1. Life consists of suffering.

2. Everything is impermanent and ever-changing.

3. The way to liberate oneself from suffering is by eliminating all desire.

4. Desire can be eliminated by following the eight-fold path.

The eight-fold path is:

1. Right understanding

2. Right thought

3. Right speech

4. Right action

5. Right livelihood

6. Right effort

7. Right awareness

8. Right meditation

The end result of a lifetime dedicated to the eight-fold path is entrance into the cycle of life, death, and rebirth (reincarnation). There is no "you" in Buddhism. Karma, human merit based on good or bad actions, will determine how many cycles one must undergo, and in what form one will be born in the next life. The Karmic cycle continues until one achieves the highest plateau of enlightenment; there he enters the state of nirvana.

Nirvana is the ultimate sphere, which followers describe as a state of nothingness, where there is no earth, water, fire, or air. It is not the sphere of infinity, or of space, or of consciousness. Nirvana is a state in which the "spirit" is finally released from the endless cycle of reincarnation. It is to the Buddhist, his ultimate "salvation."

HINDUISM

It is estimated that around 13 percent of the world's population professes to be Hindu. The origin of Hinduism can be traced back to around 1500 B.C. in present day India. It must be noted that Hinduism has no founder, doctrine, or creed. It varies widely among its adherents, but the common thread of Hinduism is the belief in reincarnation. As with Buddhism, the cycle of life, death, and reincarnation will be affected by one's karma. The ultimate salvation of the soul is achieved when one reaches the impersonal state of oneness that is called Brahman. Brahman, Hindus believe, is the ultimate state of being at one with the universe. If a person lives a good life, the soul will be born into a higher state, perhaps into the body of a Brahman bull. If a person leads an evil life, the soul will be born into a lower state, perhaps into the body of a worm. A person's reincarnation continues until he or she achieves spiritual perfection. The soul then enters a new level of existence, called moksha, from which it never returns. Like the Buddhist's nirvana, it is his salvation.

Hinduism has no single book that is the source of its doctrines. But it has many sacred writings, all of which have contributed to its fundamental beliefs. The most important include the Vedas, the Puranas, the Ramayana, the Mahabharata with its section called the Bhagavad-Gita, and the Manu Smriti.

The Hindu teachings include the caste system. The Hindu castes are grouped into five main categories, called Varnas. In order of rank, these hereditary groups are (1) Brahmans, the priests and scholars; (2) Kshatriyas, the rulers and warriors; (3) Vaisyas, the merchants and professionals; (4) Sudras, the laborers and servants; and (5) the Pariah, or the Harijans, known as the untouchables (Dalit or children of gods). Each caste system includes thousands of castes, each of which has its own rules of behavior. Through the years, the caste system has weakened somewhat, but continues to be a strong influence in Indian life. Some social distinctions have been abandoned, especially in major metropolitan cities. The fifth class is considered so low that it does not qualify for any good. Most people call it the "Untouchable" because they are forbidden to touch anyone who belongs to the four higher classes. Were a Brahmin priest to touch an untouchable, he or she must perform a ritual to wash the away the pollution. Untouchables are forced to live on the outskirts of towns and villages, and to take water downstream from the town as they may not share wells with the high class. Even today many Hindus believe that untouchables deserve this treatment because they are born into this class as a result of the bad karma earned in a previous life.

ISLAM

Approximately 20 percent of the world's population claims to be Muslim, or adherents of Islam. In A.D. 610, Muhammad claimed he had a vision from the angel Gabriel. Muhammad's ongoing revelations eventually became Islam's sacred scripture, the Koran. Muhammad preached that there was only one god, a teaching that met immediate resistance in the polytheistic culture in which he lived. An entire section of the Koran is devoted to Mary and the "man" called Jesus, the son of Mary. Islam teaches the virgin birth, sinless life, miracles, ascension and second coming of Jesus the Messiah. But, Muhammad and the Koran say that God did not have a Son. Rather, says the Koran, our Lord was merely a prophet like Muhammad, even though it says, "He was conceived by a spirit in the womb of the Virgin Mary." The Koran and the teaching of Muhammad deny that Jesus is the Son of God. It also implies that Jesus never died, but that God took Him alive into heaven, and that another person was crucified in His place. So, in the Koran there is no atonement offered for sins. Islamists believe that there are five steps to salvation. These steps are as follows:

TO RECITE THE SHADADAH

"Bear witness that there is one God but Allah and that Muhammad is His messenger."

TO PRAY

A Muslim is required to say 17 cycles of prayer each day. These cycles are said five times each day.

TO FAST

During the month of Ramadan, Muslims are expected to fast everyday.

TO GIVE ALMS

Muslims are expected to give one-fortieth of their income to the poor and needy.

TO MAKE A PILGRIMAGE

Every Muslim is expected to make at least one pilgrimage to Mecca in his lifetime. If Muslims do these five things, they believe that they will go to Paradise when they die. In other words, salvation is based on works and human effort. Islam is one of the fastest growing religions in the world. It has become the majority religion in many countries. Some report that Muslims constitute 85 percent of the population in 32 countries and between 25 and 85 percent in 11 other countries. A Muslim does not know God, but rather he obeys God. In Islam, the rules and regulations that must be followed are what please God. Yet, one can do what Allah asks his whole life and still at the end have no guarantee of acceptance. No Muslim can ever know if his good works are sufficient, or if he is predestined to Allah's favor. Salvation is mentioned several times, but not as gift. It is considered a reward for those who submit and obey.

WHICH WAY IS SALVATION?

Every other worldview is works oriented. As a Christian, it is by grace you are forgiven. Works do not earn salvation; they demonstrate it. They come as a result of what you have received as a gift of God. The grace of God is the most costly thing you can imagine.

There is no salvation in any of these other major religions. True and personal salvation is found only through Jesus Christ. And that salvation through Jesus Christ is a matter of faith.

We have a problem. Our sins separate us from God, leaving us spiritually alienated and destitute.

"All have sinned and fall short of the glory of God." Romans 3:23

It is impossible for us to find peace with God through our own efforts. Anything we do to try obtain God's favor or gain salvation is worthless and futile. Salvation is a free gift from God. He offers this gift through Jesus Christ, his Son. By laying down his life on the cross, Christ took our place and paid the ultimate price, the penalty for our sin -- death.

Jesus is our only way to God!

Jesus loves you and wants to have a personal relationship with you. God's forgiveness is available for all.

"For God so loved the world that: He gave His One and Only begotten Son, so that whosoever [everyone] *who believes in Him*

will not perish but have eternal life." John 3:16
Then how can a person have God's forgiveness, eternal life, and heaven? By trusting in Jesus as his Savior and Lord. You can do this right now by praying and asking Jesus to forgive you of your sins and inviting Jesus into your heart.

Accepting Christ is just the beginning of an eternal life with God! Get to know Him better in a number of ways:

• Follow Christ's example in baptism.

• Join a church where you can worship God and grow in your faith.

• In your church, get involved in Sunday School and Bible study.

• Begin a daily personal worship experience with God where you study the Bible and pray.

What is the economic standard among the inhabitants of the "window"?

The 40 percent of the world's population that lives in the 10/40 window subsists on an average of $1.40 per day. This is a vast area of extreme poverty that leads to waterborne illness and disease, malnutrition, high infant mortality, and a host of other problems.

Dr. Dan Reichard was living in the Philippines in the early 1980s. Shortly after arriving, he awoke during the night to the sound of something in his trashcan outside. He went to investigate and it turned out that it was not something, but rather someone. It was a child. The children would go from house to house to search trashcans for food. Food Americans would throw out would be a meal for the children's families.

Eventually Dr. Reichard realized someone else was going through his trash as well. When the garbage truck came, he could always hear it a long way off. The old diesel truck without a muffler groaned and moaned as it made its way through the streets . . . until it got to the Americans' homes. Then, just like clockwork, the engine would turn off, and the driver and the crew would begin going through the Americans' trash, piece by piece.

Dr. Reichard's wife was upset when she realized that the garbage men were taking the rotting fish and shrimp heads home with them to eat. So, she began to freeze the parts of fish and meat that her family didn't eat. When she heard the truck turn off in front of her house, she would go to the freezer and take out the food. She hand delivered it to the driver and the crew.

Every now and then, we hear someone in the United States talk about being poor. While we know that genuine poverty exists even in America, the poorest person in America is still richer than 95 percent of the people in the world. People face extreme poverty in the 10/40 window.

WHY IS INDIA SUCH A STRATEGIC PART OF THE 10/40 WINDOW?

1. The power of India's population. India's population is nearly the largest in the world, second only to China. It is estimated that the population of India, currently at more than 1 billion, will surpass that of China by 2020. This means that one out of every six people in the world today lives in India. And with a landmass only one-third the size of the continental United States, India is a very crowded country.

2. The power of India's politics. Having declared independence from the British on August 15, 1947, India is the largest functioning democracy in the world today. India maintained the power of her people, allowing them to choose their own leaders on a local and national level.

3. The power of India's protection. It is estimated that the combined military of India exceeds 1,303,000 personnel. India has also developed nuclear weapons, ensuring a critical role in maintaining regional stability.

4. The power of India's potential. India is a world player when it comes to the economy. Much of the IT (information technology) of the world today comes from Indians. India is slowly, but surely, emerging as a giant in the world of manufacturing, mining, and other areas of industry. The Indian population is industrious, adventurous, and business-minded, making an economic impact not only in India, but also around the world.

WHY IS SO MUCH OF THE WORK OF ALPHA MINISTRIES CENTERED IN INDIA?

Most of the work that Alpha Ministries is involved with is in India. The most obvious reason for this is that its founder, Cherian Mathews, is an Indian national. He was born in India, saved in India, and continues to minister in India.

Alpha Ministries currently has over 500 native missionaries in 12 Indian states and the countries of Nepal, Myanmar, Thailand, and Cambodia. Alpha Ministries has a network of church planters and global partners that we join with for one-time or long-term projects. These ministries are called MAPS, or Missionary Assistance Partnership Services. Our MAPS partners can be found in 18 Indian states and the countries of Nepal, Myanmar, Thailand, and Cambodia.

WHAT IS SIGNIFICANT ABOUT NORTH INDIA AS OPPOSED TO THE REST OF THE COUNTRY?

Notice the picture of India. See the imaginary line that runs from the bottom left to the upper right of the map? There are a few things to be aware of that will illustrate the reason Alpha's work is primarily centered in the North.

The population on the left side of the line is 700 million. The population for the smaller area on the right side of the line is 500 million. Since the population of India is 1.2 billion, that means that the 60 percent of the population lives on the left side (North India), while 40 percent of the population lives on the right side (South India).

WHAT IS WRONG WITH THIS PICTURE?

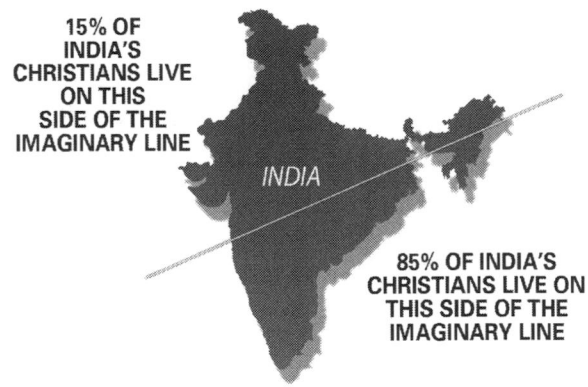

15% OF INDIA'S CHRISTIANS LIVE ON THIS SIDE OF THE IMAGINARY LINE

INDIA

85% OF INDIA'S CHRISTIANS LIVE ON THIS SIDE OF THE IMAGINARY LINE

CHANGING IT IS A MATTER OF VISION AND COMMITMENT!

This is in contrast to the ratio of Christians, the vast majority of whom live in South India. Look at the again line. Eighty-five percent of India's Christians live on the right side of the line. Only fifthteen percent of all of the Christians in India live on the left. Since the majority of India's population is in the North, why do so few of its Christians live there? There are several reasons for this:

1. Much of South India professes Christianity due to the work of early pioneer missionaries. Church tradition tells us that after the resurrection of Christ, the Apostle Thomas traveled to South India with the Gospel. Whether or not that is true is a matter of speculation. What is true is that a significant number of people in this region profess to be Christians and claim Thomas as their heritage. But, it should be noted that there is a high level of nominal churches, organizations, and Christians. Evangelical Christians make up a minority of the professing Christian community even in South India.

2. Much of the upper northeast portion of India, still on the right side of the line, is Christian. This is the area that William Carey, the "Father of Modern Missions," came to with the Gospel in the 1800s.

3. The geography and the people to the left of the line have historically been a challenge. The terrain is rough and travel is difficult and dangerous. The people are independent in their attitudes, fervent in their beliefs, and fierce in their defense of those beliefs. This area has been known for fanatical Hinduism and strong persecution of Christians.

It is in North India that over half of all the unreached people groups in the world today reside. It is here that God has placed us. It is the challenge of the ages. Just as intrepid explorers in centuries past have explored the great passages set before them, we must also set forth. We must be aware of the obstacles, but never dwell on them. We must look through them, to the other side, where millions of unreached are waiting to hear the Gospel of Jesus Christ.

Partnering in the Passage

Chapter 4

"Who will penetrate through Africa?"
- David Livingston

Dr. David Livingstone knew first-hand the vastness of Africa. As an explorer, it fascinated him. But as a missionary, it crushed him. He is said to have traveled 29,000 miles across the continent in 32 years, searching for different passages into the interior. In those dark and lonely times, he experienced a multitude of failures.

One of his greatest frustrations was the almost imperceptible growth of Christianity among the Africans. Almost as soon as he landed in 1841, he realized that the model used by European missionaries was not working. In his efforts to find a solution, he became a strong advocate in training and using natives to reach other natives. His idea was revolutionary, especially at a time when the outside world did not possess the most enlightened view of the native man.

His vision was to create a main center, or hub, that would train natives who would then radiate out across Africa. He was convinced his plan should be implemented because it was the only chance for success. He wrote the directors of the London

Missionary Society in defense of funding his vision saying in part, "It would be an immense advantage to the cause had we many such [native] agents."

Dr. Livingstone correctly realized that no European man could successfully penetrate Africa with the Gospel without the help of trained natives reaching their own people. Unfortunately, the church in England took much longer to agree with him. In the meantime, African men and women died without knowing Christ.

This did not go unnoticed by the Africans. In his journal, Dr. Livingstone recorded a particularly sad moment when he shared the Gospel with Sechele, an African chief. Sechele asked Livingstone,

"Since it is true that all who die unforgiven are lost forever, why did your nation not come to tell us of it before now? My ancestors are all gone, and none of them knew anything of what you tell me. How is this?' "

"I thought immediately," wrote Livingstone, "of the guilt of the Church, but did not confess. I told him multitudes in our own country were like himself, so much in love with their sins."

At times, the Western church has viewed the native church as inferior, even incapable of properly conducting the work of the Great Commission. But we must embrace the native church as a co-laborer with the Western church. No church can do it alone.

Native missionaries minister among their own people, in their own country, in their own language, and under their own laws. To close our hearts and ignore the potential of native missions is to put a spiritual death warrant on almost half of the world's unsaved people.

It has been said, "There is no limit to how much you can accomplish when you don't worry who gets the credit." Several years ago, Dan Marino, former quarterback for the Miami Dolphins, appeared in a commercial in which he was giving the members of his offensive line a pair of gloves at Christmas time. His line went something like this: "I want to protect the hands that protect me." In other words, Marino recognized that he, as a quarterback, couldn't be better than his offensive line allowed him to be. He might have an arm that can throw 75 yards, but it's the offensive line, the unsung heroes of any winning team, that holds back the rushing horde of defensive linemen and tacklers.

So it is with missions. The task before us is too important to fight over who gets the recognition. At stake are the souls of men. There remain hundreds of thousands of villages and tribes that have yet to hear the glorious Gospel of Jesus Christ.

Unfortunately, even God's people can struggle with their desire to receive credit. In I Samuel 30, the Israelites were at war with the Amalekites. As with any war or battle, some men were actually fighting on the frontlines, while others had to be involved in the logistical and supporting aspects of war behind the lines.

When the battle was over, there was complaining. The soldiers on the frontline didn't want to split the spoils of the victory with the soldiers who had supported them. David told them,

"For who will hearken unto you in this matter? But as his part is that goeth down to the battle, so shall his part be that tarrieth by the stuff; they shall part alike."
(I Samuel 30:24)

The same is true in missions. Both the one who goes and the one who sends are a valuable and necessary part of God's plan.

As we stand before the Judgment Seat of Christ and give an accounting of how and why we did what we did with the talents God gave us, the obedient "goer" and the obedient "sender" will each hear the words we so long for:

"Well done, thou good and faithful servant; thou hast been faithful over a few things, I will make thee ruler over many things; enter thou into the joy of the Lord."
(Matthew 25:21)

Just as surely as there will be many support people for every frontline soldier in the military, there needs to be more missions support staff behind the scenes than on the front-lines. Paul stated this truth in Romans 10:14-15a,

"How then shall they call on him in whom they have not believed? And how shall they believe in him of whom they have not heard? And how shall they hear without a preacher? And how shall they preach except they are sent?"

Paul clearly teaches that God has called some to be goers and some to be senders.

God has called us to be missions minded, and God wants us to throw ourselves wholeheartedly into missions. In many of the places we must reach out to, native missionaries are going to be the only effective way to reach the unreached. If we want to be good stewards of God's resources, we need to consider the best way to get the most out of every dollar given to missions.

We must honestly reassess our missions strategy in light of recent world changes. Something is wrong when we look at the technology at our disposal and still do missions like we did before the computer was invented. Something is wrong when we talk about loving the world, yet less than five cents out of every missions dollar goes specifically to reach the unreached.

We are not saying that we should discontinue our prayer or financial support for foreign missionaries serving in countries. We are also not saying that we should direct every missions dollar within our church to the unreached. We are advocating a strategic approach that seeks to fulfill the Great Commission in the most effective way possible.

Several years ago, while in Bombay, India, we visited a Hindu temple. It was larger than most, and there was an assortment of idols the worshippers could choose from. One group sat on the floor and chanted the mantras of their faith. They spoke to a god who did not have ears. Another group stood before a silver idol and lifted their hands in reverence in front of a god who could not see. Still others wept before lifeless idols that had no heart to care or to feel.

Each member of our group who was there that day experienced the same feelings at the same time. It wasn't a moment to take a photo or appreciate the culture. This was all out war, and the souls of millions of men and women were at stake. These worshipers, by the way, were not Christ rejecters. These were men and women who had lived their entire lives and had never, not even one time, heard about Jesus.

As we sensed the awful reality of what we were witnessing, we spontaneously joined hands in a circle of three and began praying for India. We prayed, with tears watering the soil of that great nation, that God would reveal Himself to the hundreds of millions who have yet to hear the Gospel. Jesus, the one, true God, came to save mankind from the power and penalty of their sins. The people of India have not rejected Christ. They know nothing of Christ. They are "as sheep, having no shepherd." While we thank God for the Christianization of America, our hearts break for those who live far beyond the sight of America's many church steeples and the airwaves of its many religious broadcasts.

THE FACT:

"Of the more than 135,000 North American missionaries now actively commissioned, fewer than 10,000 are working among totally unreached peoples.

Despite Christ's command to evangelize, 67% of all humans from AD 30 to the present day have never even heard his name. 96% of Christian broadcasting (radio/TV) benefits Christian nations (World C), while 0.1% benefits unevangelized nations (World A).

Worldwide Christian churches devote more than 85% of their resources on our own development. That is, only 15% of this arsenal of personnel, finance, prayer, and tools goes to bless unreached people groups.

85% of all annual scripture distribution benefits Christians (World C) and 0.4% benefits the unevangelized World A.

91% of all Christian outreach/evangelism does not target unevangelized countries, but countries that are already 95% evangelized.

818 unevangelized ethnolinguistic peoples have never been targeted by any Christian agencies ever.

The average North American Christian gives only 50 cents a week to global missions."

-Barrett and Johnson,
World Christian Trends

Passage...Crossing Borders and Fulfilling the Vision!

Pastor Mathews Cherian & Grace with Bennie & Finny in 1969.

Today the family has grown to five sons, their wives, one daughter, her husband, and twenty grandchildren.
Reaching the unreached and telling the untold!

Taking the gospel to the neediest and remotest regions

Training Frontline Leaders to Plant Churches Where No Church Exists!

Glorifying God among unreached peoples by initiating church-planting.

Alpha Bible Institute

Training and equipping natives in Burma to be effective church planters.

Bringing the Gospel to the Unreached and Unengaged...

Church Planting Movement in Nepal.

Church Planting Movement in South Asia among the Mavchi people groups.

Furthering the Gospel by planting churches where no church exists in South Asia.

Living for the Passage

Chapter 5

"I will lay my bones by the Ganges that India might know there is one who cares."
- Alexander Duff

PASSION FOR THE PASSAGE

The morning of November 21, 2005, I was packing for my afternoon flight back to the USA when I received a phone call that sent chills down my spine. The police told me they had discovered a young man's body by railroad tracks in a very remote area of South Asia. The police claimed the man was one of Alpha Ministries' church planters and said that I needed to make the final identification.

My heart was breaking as I rushed with colleagues to the site to confirm and gather details. Unfortunately, we were able to positively identify the man as one of our young and dynamic church-planters, A.R.

---

*In order to maintain the safety of our church planters, it is necessary to abbreviate names and change certain details throughout this book.

A.R. was 22 years old and planted churches with zeal in the state of Gujarat. A graduate of Alpha Bible College, he moved to an unreached village to start a pioneering work among hostile and predominantly Hindu natives.

He suffered many personal attacks during his young life. He was stripped naked and subjected to humiliating and debilitating physical beatings for the cause of the Gospel, enduring them all with joy. For him, it was a badge of honor to suffer for Christ, and with pride he would raise the banner,

"For me to live is Christ, and to die is gain." (Phil 1:21)

Once, when asked how he endured those beatings, he replied, "I only felt the first beating, and then I felt as if the Lord had put a blanket over me and all I could hear was the sound of the beatings, but no pain."

Just a few days before his death, A.R. and I were together for our annual IMPACT Church Planters Conference in Anand, India. He had left the conference with a renewed passion and energy to preach the Gospel to his people. He was traveling by train with other pastors back to his home when four young men came into the train cabin. They told A.R. to come with them to discuss something. He left with them and never came back. One of the pastors who was with A.R. got off the train at his stop, thinking that A.R. would make it home. Nothing was known about the incident until the next morning when A.R.'s body was found on the tracks and the police contacted our office.

A.R. was found mutilated; only his head was intact. The police informed us that they had to put the body parts in a sack since it was cut to bits. His belt, shoes, and handkerchief were found strewn about 40 feet from the track, an obvious sign it wasn't a train accident. We went to the medical examiner's office for the autopsy report, but the police withheld it from us. Foul play was involved and they did not want to disclose the details.

Here was a true martyr who considered it a privilege to be counted worthy to suffer for the name of Christ. Threats and oppositions were no match to A.R.'s commitment to his Savior. At the young age of 22, he had accomplished the task he was entrusted with. He ran the race and finished the course, remaining unmoved and faithful to his calling even to the point of death. Christ's passion so gripped his heart that he was willing to pay the ultimate price. Christ's passion, that the world might know and love His father, was also the passion of AR.

In John 4:4, it is said Christ, "had to pass through Samaria." (NAS) Jesus, being a Jew, knew that "good Jews" despised the Samaritans. A Jew would go out of his way and walk farther than he had to, just to avoid going into Samaria. He did not want even the dust of that land and people to contaminate his sandals.

But, Jesus walked through Samaria because He came to seek and save that which was lost. Jesus said,

"God so loved the world that He gave His only begotten Son, that whosoever believeth in Him should not perish but have everlasting life." (John 3:16)

Jesus knew full well that,

"The wages of sin is death but the gift of God is eternal life through Jesus Christ our Lord." (Romans 6:23)

Jesus willingly left heaven's glory to walk as a man among sinful men. He "contaminated" His sinless feet upon the dust of this sin-cursed planet to save mankind from their sin. Before His passion on the cross, Jesus came as a passionate missionary from heaven to earth.

Today, the increasing persecution of the church hasn't diminished its passion in Asia. Trials continue to abound in the ministry. Our native missionaries weather one storm after another, brought by a determined and persistent opposition. Many of them have been singled out as targets in a futile attempt to suppress the growing voice of the Gospel. Christ's passion has so gripped our native missionaries' hearts, that though they face intense persecution in the form of assaults and emotional attacks, none of these afflictions have bent their steel resolve.

S.P. is one of many of our church planters who have endured many hardships and even physical torture for the sake of Christ. He was away in a village proclaiming the Gospel when an anonymous caller informed S.P.'s neighbor that his body had been found. The stunned neighbor then informed S.P.'s wife, who frantically called the Alpha Ministries' missions office. Our staff rushed to help. After our unsuccessful search that lasted well into the night, an oblivious S.P. showed up at his home, to the bewilderment of all of us. It turned out to be a cruel and vicious prank played on the unsuspecting wife of a missionary. A few days later, yet another missionary and his family were targets of the same kind of attack.

Church planter O.P. was leading worship when a group of militant Hindus attacked his small congregation. They began ransacking the church, pulling down and burning posters, Scripture verses, and anything remotely "Christian". O.P. and his wife were forcibly taken to a nearby police station to face a tirade of false accusations including allegations of bribing people with the intent to convert them to Christianity. False witnesses were brought in to testify against them. Subsequently, the police arrested them to appease the angry mob.

During late evening hours on weekdays in India, prayer meetings and Bible studies take place in believers' homes. The militants target such gatherings. They barge into homes and physically abuse the men in front of their wives and children, creating a commotion while a crowd gathers. Then, when the police arrive, the militants accuse the Christian leaders of converting the residents. The men are handed over to the police under false charges. Most of the time, the women and children are then left alone to defend themselves. It is a horrific mental and emotional torture to families.

In one northern Indian state, the local government is working vehemently on an agenda to stop churches that are actively involved in church planting. The government has begun to notice the increasing growth of churches in this state during the last ten years, and recognized that these new churches are the result of missionary activity undertaken by church-planting agencies like Alpha Ministries. In a sinister move, the government has declared that it will only recognize the Episcopal Church. They realize that the traditional Episcopal Church does not evangelize and has no active missionary agenda, thereby posing no threat. This is clearly a tactic engaged by the enemy to specifically target those ministries involved in spreading the Gospel. Acting in coordination with Hindu militant organizations, they have begun a fresh wave of attacks against new and growing churches in the region. Their aim is to intimidate pastors and pressure newly converted Christians by subjecting them to humiliation.

In years past, four Alpha Churches were burned, and pastors were brutally attacked. It became difficult for Christians to even conduct regular prayer meetings at home. The anti-Christian forces targeted places of worship, challenging their followers to burn them to the ground. This is a country with several temples in each village, and over 800 million people worshiping 338 million gods and goddesses. Each month, new gurus and new sites are being invented for worship. This is a country where every home has an altar or a shrine to its beloved deity. These are people who worship millions upon millions of gods, yet they do not want anyone to worship or follow the one true God, Jesus Christ.

Forty-five years ago, a young couple left Kerala, a state in South India. They left their home and community to travel 1,500 miles to reach the unreached and untold millions in North India. My father and mother stepped out in faith, obeying the voice of God. The passion of Christ motivated their hearts to reach North India with the glorious message of His love and salvation. Christ's passion, the missionary's passion, gripped their hearts and enabled them to face hardship, starvation, and persecution.

It is normal to be concerned with our safety as well as the safety of our loved ones. Even as Christians, we have our fears. Every time I return from a mission trip, one of my friends will take a deep breath, give a sigh of relief, and say, "Man, you are home!" He will often tell me, "Bennie, people love you, please try to stay home. You could get sick, be persecuted…even be killed! When you are away and I hear about an airplane crash, my heart submerges into fear. Bennie, I know God is in control, but we love you."

The world of our enemy is a fearful place, but when we are filled with God's passion, we are no longer bound to fear. We are bound to God Himself! We cannot cage ourselves, trying to prolong the number of days God has set for each of us. More important than safety, more important than beatings and torture, more important than death itself is the very will of God, leading to a passion for the unreached.

PURPOSE IN THE PASSAGE

R.G. seemed too frail to live, much less to be a preacher. He had grown up in a poor family and had suffered from malnourishment most of his life. His body was racked with ailments, including tuberculosis, as a result.

R.G. came to the Alpha Bible Institute in Baroda, North India determined to become a preacher. He lacked the physical strength to keep up the rigorous workload of a Bible school student and he was unable to ride a bike or walk great distances to minister in local villages. Still, he had a tremendous passion for the lost and he was determined to fulfill what he believed was God's purpose for his life. For much of the time, R.G. was unable to stay in the dorm or attend classes due to his sicknesses. Eventually, he had to move into the home of my mother, Grace, to be fed and cared for during long periods.

Even though he was very ill, R.G. began fasting and praying, asking God to fulfill his dream to be a preacher of the Gospel. He didn't share his dream or his fasting with his fellow students. He feared that they would rebuke him for not eating when he was sick.

Once R.G. was officially diagnosed with tuberculosis, he had to withdraw from school and return to his home. Still believing in God's purpose and in the power of prayer and fasting, his eyes were drawn to a high mountain that overlooked his village. Within his heart, he believed God was telling him that the answer to his prayers was at the top of that mountain.

Early one morning he began the journey that would change his life and the lives of a people he had never met. He struggled to climb to the top of that mountain. When he finally reached the peak, he felt a surge of physical and spiritual strength. In the days that followed, God completely healed him of his tuberculosis. R.G. began to share Christ with the unreached people who lived on that mountain. Soon, they followed Christ in baptism and began to serve God.

Today, the congregation of the remote Alpha church, sitting on top of that high mountain, has more than 60 members. R.G. is their pastor and although he looks frail, the Holy Spirit is using him in a mighty way.

R.G. realized God's purpose for his life when, in obedience, he walked through the Passage to reach those on the other side.

MISSION FOR THE PASSAGE

In the household of Pothan and Rachael Mathai (Mathews), January 30, 1939 wasn't a day of "firsts." Rachael would give birth to a son on that day but he would be the eighth child in a family that would eventually have nine children. Pothan was a hardworking farmer in the state of Kerala, South India. By India's standards, he was a blessed man to own his own land and to be the father of a large family.

Pothan breathed a word of thanks for the safe arrival of his newborn son. After all, every healthy son was a blessing to a busy farmer who appreciated the extra help in the fields, even if it would be a while in the making. But he did not pray to one of the gods or goddesses of Hinduism. His prayer was directed to the God of his Christian faith.

The Mathews family had been members of the Christian church in India for as many generations as they could remember. As is customary for Indian Christians, they would have, no doubt, attributed their Christian roots to the Apostle Thomas himself. It is a church tradition that after the resurrection of Christ, Thomas evangelized India, especially southern India. Christianity, though lived out very nominally, was the faith of much of India and the Mathews family as well.

The eighth child was named Cherian. It would have been impossible for these proud parents to hold their newborn in their arms and imagine that one day he would impact his nation for God. They could not dream that he would become a human instrument of moving India from fear and superstition to the light and freedom of the Gospel of Christ. Little did they know that Cherian, who would work with his father in the fields, would one day hear the unmistakable voice of his heavenly Father say to him,

"Lift up your eye, and look on the fields; for they are white already to harvest." (John 4:35b)

It was not the harvest of his earthly father's fields, but the harvest of human souls for his heavenly Father.

As young Cherian Mathews grew, his father had his own plans for his son. Pothan wanted his son to receive an education, join the army, and begin earning a living. With the money Cherian earned, he could help support his family.

One day in 1958, an eighteen-year-old Cherian was looking for a job. While he was waiting for a bus, he heard the sound of music. Looking around, he realized that it was coming from a group of Christians conducting an open-air meeting. As he sat and listened from the bus stop, he found himself captivated by the message of the speaker.

These Christians at the meeting were not like the Christians Cherian knew. They were not like the ones who worshiped in his father's church. Nor were they like his father or anyone else in his family. There was a joy and a sense of celebration among these believers. The speaker said it wasn't enough just to call oneself a Christian. He told them that Jesus did not come to die on the cross just so that they would go to church. Jesus died and rose again so that man's sin might be forgiven and that he might spend eternity in heaven. The speaker told the crowd that Jesus said, "Ye must be born again." These words pierced young

Cherian's heart deeply.

When the music finished and the street preacher concluded his message, Cherian left the bus stop and walked over to the meeting. He opened up his heart to the preacher, and that same day, he opened up his heart to receive Christ as His Savior.

The thought of finding a job, at least on that day, was forgotten. Cherian rushed home as fast as he could to tell his father the wonderful news. But instead of seeing his father's face fill with joy, it twisted in outrage. Pothan threatened to throw his son out of the house if he continued to associate with "fanatics." Even though Pothan was a Christian, his faith was nominal and he couldn't tolerate a level of Christianity that would interfere with his, or his sons, lives. Cherian remembered the day that his brother became a Christian and was also threatened by his father. His brother had left home because of it, but Cherian still wanted to please his father.

So he stayed at home and continued to work with his father in the fields. Little did Pothan know that Cherian was secretly fellowshipping with other Christian believers. With his newfound brothers and sisters, Cherian was studying the Bible and growing in knowledge. He was sharing his joy with his fellow Christians and he was sharing the Gospel with his community.

On the day that Cherian was baptized, he told his mother all about it. Eventually, the news of his baptism and public confession became known in the community and his father heard about it. Again, Cherian's father was incensed. This time, Pothan told Cherian to take everything he owned and leave. He had to leave the only home he had ever known.

Cherian left his parents and home with only his Bible and a few clothes. Soon, he was sleeping on sidewalks. On those lonely nights, Cherian would use his Bible as a pillow for his head and fall asleep covered only by the hands of God. Sometimes he would sneak into the backyard of his father's house and wait until his mother snuck him some food to eat.

It was a hard time, but Cherian sought God's direction for his life, and his struggles built his faith and trust in God. Cherian relied on Him to provide his every need. He was blessed to meet a young, godly girl named Grace. They fell in love and were married. God also opened the door for Cherian to begin attending a local Bible school. When he graduated, he answered the missionary call to leave the safe confines of South India and go to the state of Gujarat in North India.

North India has always been regarded as a dark and dangerous area…a spiritual desert. Even in evangelistic circles, missions to the unknown and frightening people groups of the North were regarded as strange. It was unheard of for someone to leave South India and travel to North India as a missionary. Pastor Mathews and Grace were pioneers in every sense of the word. They sought to find the "Passage to the Unreached."

My father Cherian and my mother Grace took me when I was an infant and stepped off a train in the city of Baroda, Gujarat in 1965. It was like arriving in a different country. They didn't speak a word of the local language. The people dressed differently, ate different foods, and practiced different customs. Cherian and his family were strangers in a city of one million people. They had no financial support from South India. In fact, many of their friends doubted they would ever see them alive again.

Their first need was shelter. But, they had very little money, not enough to rent a home. As it was, they barely had enough money to buy food. But soon after arriving, Grace saw an empty house in a full neighborhood. She asked the owner why it wasn't rented. The owner told her that evil spirits haunted it and so they could not find anyone who was willing to live there. Grace knew that evil spirits were no match for her God. She asked the owner how much he would charge for rent. Unbelievably, it was only a fraction of the average rent. They dedicated the house to God and never had a problem with the evil spirits. The Mathews' knew that God had provided that home as a place to raise their family and to begin what would become the Alpha Bible Church in Baroda.

Their next challenge was learning the Gujarati language. They were Christians in the middle of an unfriendly Hindu population. They could not find a willing tutor and they didn't have access to any books that would help. One night, there was the sound of a loud explosion outside the house. My father ran outside to see what it was. He saw that a large transformer had exploded and caught on fire. Children were pointing up to the fire and yelling, "Aag!" It only took a moment for him to realize "aag" meant "fire". Aag was the first Gujarati word that my parents learned, but more importantly they had found their tutors: the neighborhood children.

As time went on, Cherian learned Gujarati and he was soon able to minister to the people of Baroda. For what seemed like a long time, he would conduct Sunday morning services in his living room with his only congregation members: his family. But it was the beginning of the Alpha Bible Church, and before long, Cherian lead his first converts to Christ.

God not only blessed the church with growth, He blessed the Mathews' family with growth as well. Soon, Finny, Glory, Denny, Davis, Jimmy, and Lovely were added to the family. Including me, there were now seven children. At the age of three, my sister Glory lived up to her name and went to be with the Lord of All Glory, having suffered from typhoid and pneumonia.

The Alpha Bible Church in Baroda was in its infancy. Though

the numbers were few, God was preparing that simple family and that small church in the midst of that mighty nation, to launch a great native missionary expedition of faith. That was the birth of the Alpha Missionary Movement. It was born in the heart of God and in the heart of a mission- driven man, Cherian Mathews.

THE PASSAGE MOVEMENT

All it takes for one man's vision and mission to become a movement is for someone to follow. But, as is the case with most men whom God has greatly used, Cherian did not begin with the goal of starting a movement. Pastor Mathews and Grace, affectionately known as Mother Grace, were just doing what God told them to do. There was no thought of a movement. There was no conscious effort to develop a legacy or secure their place in Church history. But God had plans beyond what the Mathews' could have ever imagined.

Two factors caused the birth of a missions-driven movement from a missions-driven man: discipleship and evangelism. The personal fervor in which Cherian embarked on the task of discipling was motivated by the conviction that discipleship had played a tremendous role in his life and walk with Christ. It was in the early days of Cherian's faith that God allowed him to be surrounded by believers who were willing to love, care for, nurture, and disciple the eighteen-year-old farmer's son who had been thrown out of his home. Discipleship was also important to him because he knew from his study of the Scriptures that discipleship was important to God. Cherian's obedience to Christ and His Word caused him to see the priority that God places, not only on the salvation of a soul, but on the discipleship of that soul as well. The result was that God began to entrust the most precious commodity in the world to pastor Mathews and the Alpha Bible Church in Baroda: the eternal souls of men.

The second reason that Cherian saw his vision spread into a mission-driven movement was due to was the fervor with which he sought to preach Christ and plant churches among the unreached people groups of North India. Even in the early days, when most pastors would be content working on building a great home church, Cherian always looked beyond the borders of his city.

Often times, God would allow Pastor Mathews to lead people to Christ who had family in the outlying areas of the city. The new converts, as they grew in the grace and knowledge of Jesus Christ, would become increasingly burdened for their own family and friends. Pastor Mathews was equally burdened for the unreached outside the city. Several times a month he would leave Baroda to travel, usually on foot, to the tribal areas that surrounded his home. As time went on, God allowed Pastor Mathews to see many come to Christ from many different villages and people groups.

It was the merging of his commitment to discipleship and missions that drew Pastor Mathews back to the villages and their converts over and over again. It was the result of that commitment that believers matured and churches were planted in areas where no church had ever existed before. Soon there were 12 churches. This was the first missionary movement in the state of Gujarat, North India. Thus, the movement was called the Alpha Missionary Movement of North India.

As these newly planted churches began to grow, God called their new members into the ministry. These men would stay in the home of Pastor and Mrs. Mathews for days at a time, studying the Word of God and absorbing Cherian's vision. On weekends, the men would go to the surrounding neighborhoods to preach Christ and plant churches. As the vision to reach North India grew larger than the state of Gujarat and even North India itself, the name was changed to Alpha Ministries. This movement was the fire that began to burn and spread from village to village in a land that had never heard the Gospel of Jesus Christ before.

As the numbers of men who desired to study God's Word and become missionary church planters began to increase, so did the demands on the home and time of Pastor Mathews. It was decided that part of the house would be designated as a place for the students to sleep and study. Their home was to become the Alpha Bible School in Baroda. The school was a place where students could come and study in a one-year program. Over the years, the school developed into an institute that is still training men and women today.

As time went on, it became impossible to disciple as many pastors, leaders, and planters as wanted to spend time with Pastor Mathews. Not only did the Alpha family continue to grow, but requests came from church leaders from all over North India who desired to spend time with Pastor Mathews and to learn of his vision. It was out of that hunger and the training at Amsterdam that God began the first IMPACT Conference in 1990.

ALPHA GLOBAL IMPACT CHURCH PLANTERS CONFERENCE

The IMPACT Church Planters Conference is a key component in the success of not only Alpha Ministries, but also the vast majority of the evangelical work that is going on in North India and Asia. At the heart of Alpha Ministries has always been the commitment to train the trainers. We must build leaders who build the church. This is discipleship of leadership. Someone once said, "Leadership is something that is more 'caught' than 'taught.'" If that is so, and we believe that it is, then that is part of the reason why God has blessed this ministry.

Paul said of Timothy in II Timothy 1:5, "When I call to remembrance the unfeigned faith that is in thee, which dwelt first in thy grandmother Lois and thy mother Eunice; and I am persuaded that is in thee also."

Paul was saying to Timothy, "The qualities I see in you, I also saw in your mother and your grandmother." In other words, Timothy "caught" the faith of his mother and grandmother. Those who attend the IMPACT conference have the opportunity to "catch" the vision of Pastor Mathews and others who have made Alpha Ministries the ministry it is today.

For those participants who register ahead of time, Alpha Ministries pays for everything (transportation, food, lodging, and all books and materials). Alpha Ministries has assumed full financial responsibility since the very first conference, believing God would meet the needs. The financial responsibility is great, but otherwise many of the pastors and church leaders could not afford to attend the conference.

It is still required that every month church planter must meet at their regional headquarters for two days each month for a church planters meeting.

On the first day of the meeting, the pastors and planters spend the day together and enter into a time of prayer and fasting. They also embark on an intense, ongoing study of the Word of God. After the study, they are tested on biblical assignments that were given the previous month.

On the second day, they give a progress report of their churches and mission field. They share about their triumphs and tragedies on the frontline. Each church planter is responsible for establishing at least two to four new areas or villages to preach in. Some of these will become churches as God leads. The second day is a time to discuss plans and problems, and a time for these pastors to seek advice, encouragement, and direction.

The last day is a day of feasting and praise. The pastors are fed wonderful meals and they spend time praising God through testimony and songs. As the pastors leave and return to their work, they are encouraged and are again aware that they are not alone. They are part of a fellowship of other men who are accomplishing the same work.

Alpha Ministries is still doing what it has done from day one: placing an emphasis on one-on-one discipleship and church planting. While it may be said that the Alpha Ministries movement began in the heart of a mission-driven man, in reality, it began in the heart of a mission-driven God.

Living for the Passage involves more than an intellectual assent to the idea that the unreached must be reached. It is living a life full of passion and purpose for those who are lost. It is a life driven by the mission to tell the untold. It is a movement spreading the Gospel like a wildfire.

"The core of the unreached people of our world live in a rectangular shaped window. Often called the Resistance Belt, the window extends from West Africa to East Asia, from 10 degrees north to 40 degrees north of the equator.
This specific region, which has increasingly become known as The 10/40 Window, encompasses the majority of the world's Muslims, Hindus, Buddhists -
billions of spiritually impoverished souls."
-AD2000 & Beyond

"Jesus is not coming back to take a crowd.
He is coming to get His Bride (the Church)"
–Pastor Cherian Mathews
Founder & President
Alpha Ministries

Passage Misconceptions

Chapter 6

"Any church that is not seriously involved in helping fulfill the Great Commission has forfeited its biblical right to exist."
- Oswald J. Smith

Where is the outcry of God's people who hear the screams of 50,000 people per day as they fall into a dark eternity? How can there be such a disparity between our work among the already reached and the yet unreached? Why doesn't every church in America adopt an unreached people group and pray for God to send someone to tell them about His Son, Jesus Christ? Why doesn't every church determine to give more to reach the unreached people groups of the world?

These are difficult questions to answer. Why isn't the church more effective? A lifetime of experience in missions has taught me that it is not because of what we do or do not know...it is because of what we think we know.

MISCONCEPTION NUMBER 1:

"Missions is optional, not mandatory."

Every now and then, when I'm speaking to churches on

missions, someone will approach me at the end of the service and say something like this: "I appreciate what you had to say, but we're not that kind of church."

What kind of church is that, I wonder to myself?

They may mean that their church places its emphasis on discipleship, rather than on missions. Perhaps they mean that their church is a "teaching" church and not a "reaching" church. It's as if God gave churches the privilege of walking through a spiritual buffet line and allowed them to pick and choose the parts of His work they wanted to obey.

When someone says, "We are not that kind of church," I want to say, "You mean an obedient church?" A church that is not committed to the Great Commission and worldwide evangelism is not an obedient church. The Great Commission is a command, not a suggestion. Someone said, "If you take missions out of church, then there is no church." Missions is the reason the church exists.

MISCONCEPTION NUMBER 2:

"Native missionaries cannot do the work as well as or as lasting as American missionaries can."

The truth is that native missionaries can do the work as well as American missionaries, and they are doing it every day. There are tremendous advantages in using natives. They know the language, people, and customs. The cost of support is only a fraction of what an overseas missionary requires, and the turn-over rate is much lower. We in America have been blessed with tremendous Bible colleges, seminaries, resources, and a nurturing and mentoring infrastructure that surpasses anything that this world has ever seen. But that does not mean we are the only ones who can do the job.

When you hear the word "natives", do you think of a primitive tribe of people, running around in body paint and throwing spears at every bush that moves? Native means inhabitant, national, resident, or dweller of a region. When Paul, Barnabas, and other missionaries in the book of Acts went to different countries, every one of their converts was a native preacher. Native preachers have always been God's plan. It was never God's plan for one nation, regardless of how blessed or how competent, to go into other countries and permanently pastor churches.

MISCONCEPTION NUMBER 3:

"Jerusalem, Judea, Samaria, and the uttermost parts of the world are literal, geographical locations."

A missionary friend confessed to me that even after he was involved in full-time missions, he would read Acts 1:8,

"But ye shall receive power, after that the Holy Ghost is come upon you; and ye shall be witnesses unto me both in Jerusalem, and in all Judea, and in Samaria and unto the uttermost part of the earth."

When he did, he would see the three geographical target areas as just that, geographical locations. Then one day, it dawned on him. These weren't the names of cities or countries. These weren't just places on a map. These were people. Jesus was telling His church, "Be a witness of my life, my death, and my resurrection to everyone who lives in Jerusalem. Be a witness to every one of them, regardless of his religion or his status in life. To the young and the old, tell every one of them that I love them and that I came to this world to die for them that they, through my sacrificial death on the cross, might have the gift of everlasting life and live forever with me in heaven."

Jesus was saying to the church and is saying to us today, "Go to the people who live outside of your neighborhoods, your Judea, and stop by every house and give them a message from me. Tell them I love them. Tell them I am the one who created them, and I am the one who knows each of them by name. Personally invite them to live in heaven when they die so they can enjoy the very purpose for which I created them."

Jesus Christ is saying that we should go to our Samaria and deliver this message to them: "Though the world looks upon you with disgust, and you are despised by those around you, please know that God loves you with an everlasting love. Before you were even created, the God-Head determined that They would create mankind, yes, even the Samaritans, that they might worship God and thus fulfill the ultimate purpose of love. Yet, in Their omniscience, They knew man would sin. But, God the Father determined to provide a way in which mankind might be reconciled to Him."

"Jesus said that He would go and die on the cross as the perfect sacrifice for sin and be raised on the third day to declare that He is indeed Lord. The Holy Spirit said that He would convict men of their sin and be the Divine instrument of the new birth. The Holy Spirit also said that He would indwell and fill believers to live a godly life that would be pleasing to their Father and empower them to take His message to every person in the entire world."

To the people who live beyond the city limits of Jerusalem and the regions of Judea and Samaria (that is you and me by the way), Jesus says, "Go far beyond the walls of safety and security. Take this message from heaven to those who speak other languages and practice different customs that seem strange and even repulsive. Tell them that you have come to obey Psalm 105:1:

'Make known among the nations what He has done'

Tell them that,

'(We) are a light for the Gentiles that (we) might bring salvation to the ends of the earth.'" (Isaiah 49:6)

"Tell them that I am planning a great day of celebration, and I want them to come. Let them know that it is my plan that on that day of celebration that they be there and be a part of what John foresaw in Revelation 7:9-10 when he wrote,

'After this I beheld and lo, a great multitude, which no man could number, of all nations (ethnic groups), and kindreds (families), and people, and tongues (languages), stood before the throne and before the Lamb, clothed with white robes, and palms in their hands; And cried with a loud voice saying, Salvation to our God which sitteth upon the throne and unto the Lamb.'"

Yes, the world that God loves and commissions us to go to is not a list of places. It is people for whom Christ died.

MISCONCEPTION NUMBER 4:

"'Nations' are countries."

Jesus said in Matthew 28:19- 20,

"Go ye therefore, and teach all nations, baptizing them in the name of the Father, and of the Son, and of the Holy Ghost: Teaching them to observe all things whatsoever I have commanded you: and lo, I am with you always, even unto the end of the world. Amen."

From this command we recognize many things, not the least of which is that Christ wants us to go to "all nations." But what does "all nations" mean? We think of a nation as being a self-governing and self-ruling organization of people who have recognized borders, i.e., a country. If that definition is true, then there was really only one nation in Jesus' day. The nation would have been the Roman Empire. If our modern definition of nation is what Jesus meant, then the moment that the very first believer was baptized and began to be discipled, the Great Commission would have been fulfilled.

The number of nations in any particular period of history has varied. In the twenty-first century, we are told that there are 237 separate nations in the world. Can we rightly say that if we had at least one baptized and discipled believer in each of those 237 nations that the Great Commission would technically be fulfilled? Is baptizing and discipling one believer in each nation our goal? Should that be our goal if we desire to fulfill the Great Commission in our lifetime?

The truth is that the word nation in the Bible doesn't mean nation as we think of it today. The Greek word for nation in our New Testament is the word ethne. Ethne, while it is usually translated nation, means "an ethnic division." We use the term "ethnic group" to define a specific and distinct group of people. An ethnic or people group can be defined as a group of people who share customs, religions, a common language, and more.

Take the United States for instance: we are one nation made up of many nations, or ethnic groups. So, while the United States of America is one nation, we are many nations (ethnos). When Jesus told us to go into all nations, He was telling us to take His message to every ethnic or people group of the world.

It is estimated that there are 24,000 nations (in the biblical meaning of the word) in the world today. While estimates vary, it is estimated that about 6,000 of these nations do not have a Gospel witness among them. Thus, they are the unreached people groups. The bottom line is that there are far more nations in the world today than the 237 officially recognized independent nations that we find on our map.

It is possible that this misconception has led to the Church to assume the "finish line" is closer than it actually is. But, the finish line will not be reached until every ethnic group has been reached.

MISCONCEPTION NUMBER 5:

"We are losing the war."

If you listen to some in the missions community, you might believe that the church started off with a bang in the days of the Apostles, but has slowly been running out of steam ever since. To some, it seems that the number of people who are receiving Christ is far less than the number of people who are dying without Him. We are faced with a booming population in our time in history: of all people who have ever walked this earth, 80 percent are living today.

The truth is that statistically we are winning. The ratio of people who profess to know Christ is greater today than it has ever been before, and the ratio continues to grow. There is a great movement going on in many unreached people groups in India and China. Consider this: in A.D. 100, at the end of the Apostolic Age, the ratio of believers to non-believers was about 1:360. Today, the ratio is about 1:9. And of these unbelievers, only four of the nine are from unreached people groups. How close are we to (potentially and realistically) fulfilling the Great Commission? May we suggest that all it will take to begin is for one obedient church to adopt one unreached people group and make God's priority their priority? Will your church be that one?

MISCONCEPTION NUMBER 6:

"God told me I didn't have to."

This is perhaps the subtlest of all misconceptions. After all, one will never hear a believer say, "I don't care what Christ said! I am not going to get involved in missions!" One won't hear a church say, "It doesn't matter to us if people die without Christ!" No Bible-believing pastor will stand at his pulpit and say, "God hasn't told us to go into all the world."

So, if people aren't saying these things, but far too many churches are practicing them, what is the problem? The problem is that Christians have somehow come to believe that God has released them from the responsibility of missions. Some theological misunderstandings are blatantly untrue and will cause us to deny our responsibility to God and to the unsaved. Here are three examples of misunderstandings or, "God told me I didn't have to" misconceptions:

"God wouldn't send people to hell who have never heard the Gospel."

Charles Haddon Spurgeon said, "Someone asked, 'Will the heathen who have never heard the Gospel be saved?' It is more a question, with me, whether we-who have the Gospel and fail to give it to those who have not-can be saved."

The misconception that an ignorant soul is not liable for his sins somehow gives comfort to the hearts of men and women who don't bend a knee or lift a hand to spread the Gospel. If that were actually the case, it would be better to not tell them and let them go to heaven when they die, rather than risk them rejecting the Gospel and going to hell.

What the Bible does teach is that,

"All [all means all] have sinned and come short of the glory of God." (Romans 3:23)

"The wages of sin is death." [eternal separation from God].... (Romans 6:23a)

"Neither is there salvation in any other; for there is none other name under heaven given among men, whereby we must be saved." (Acts 4:12)

"I am the way and the truth and the life. No man [whether or not he has heard the Gospel] comes to the Father but by me." (John 14:6)

Feelings, wishes, and misconceptions aside, those who die without Christ are eternally lost.

Allow me to illustrate: A person is walking down the street. While walking, he looks over to see smoke coming out of the window of one of the houses. He can even hear cries for help coming from the building. But, he continues on his stroll and upon reading the newspaper the next morning learns that two people died in the fire. He becomes furious and writes a letter to the editor, criticizing the local fire department for not doing their job.

Was it the fault of the fire department that two people died in the house fire? Or was it the fault of the person who saw the problem, knew what he should do, but ignored his responsibilities? If the unreached die without ever hearing about Christ, is it God's fault? It is the fault of you and me who see the problem, know what we should do, but ignore our responsibility.

Christ has done all that He needs to do to save every man, woman, boy, and girl on planet Earth. It is our responsibility to go into the "burning homes" and warn the inhabitants of the impending danger. The songwriter wrote, "Send the light… Send the light…" We who have the Light must be sent as the Light.

"Since God already knows who will or won't be saved, it doesn't matter if we send missionaries!"

Let us say at the outset that this misconception is more a matter of attitude than theology. God does know who will and who won't be saved. He is God and God is omniscient.

He also does not need us to accomplish His stated mission of redeeming men from every nation. But God is sovereign, and in His sovereignty, He has chosen to involve man in his process of redeeming them. He has deemed man to be the human instrument of sharing the good news of redemption, and He has deemed the church to be keeper of the "keys" (representing access and authority) of the very doors of heaven (Matthew 16:19). We can share the keys with a lost and dying world, or we can disobey and choose not to. It is the choice given to us by a Sovereign God.

Spurgeon said, "I know that God has elected some to heaven and some are not of the elect. If God had drawn a big X on the back of those who would respond to the Gospel and not on the backs of those who would reject the Gospel, then I would lift up the coats of everyone I meet to see if they have an X on their back before I witness to them. Since He has not, I will witness to each and every person that I meet because I am not God."

"God's plan for the 'heathen' is that they be saved in the tribulation."

This misconception is based on faulty eschatology, or the study of future events. We know Christ is coming to rapture His church at some point in the future. We also know God has reserved a point in history when He will pour out His wrath upon the earth and the inhabitants of it. This outpouring of God's wrath is commonly called the tribulation. We know that there is coming a period of 1,000 years in which Christ Himself will rule and reign on this earth from His throne in Jerusalem. This period of time is called the millennial kingdom.

Much debate surrounds the timeline of some of these events. Some believe God will save the unreached people groups during the tribulation, but not necessarily before the rapture. This belief can alleviate the responsibility to reach all of the unreached people groups of the world before the rapture. In other words, "Let's put our responsibility for world evangelism off. Let the tribulation saints do it."

The bottom line is this: any theology that negates, nullifies, shifts responsibility, or in any way causes us to feel anything less than sole responsibility for evangelizing to every person on earth is not correct theology.

MISCONCEPTION NUMBER 7:

"We have enough unsaved people right here to worry about."

Even without knowing where you live and how great the need is around you, I can safely say that, yes, there are many unsaved right in your own neighborhood. And yes, you must witness to them.

But Jesus told us in Acts 1:8 that while we are to witness to the unsaved around us, we are also to be conscious of the fact that there are others outside our neighborhood who need to be reached as well. We are responsible for both groups. We can't wait until all of the people in our Jerusalem, Judea, and Samaria are saved, baptized, and discipled before we become actively involved in ministering to those in the "uttermost parts of the world," because that time will never come.

I remember when my brother, Finny, was pastoring a church in Southern Virginia. On my second trip to the church, about a year after he started pastoring, I looked at the church sign and saw a big difference. The earlier sign only had the name of the church and a pointer. Now there was a new sign and it not only had the church name but a new phrase: "Reaching Locally and Globally." The church has been in existence for a long time, but they had only recently realized the true importance of missions.

MISCONCEPTION NUMBER 8:

"If we start emphasizing missions around the world, it will take our focus off of our local church."

Common sense tells us that if we want to have more of anything later, then we must spend less of it today. This is the basic principle of saving. And that principle, by the way, is generally true.

But when we apply this principle to human beings, we find a difference. For example, the principle would dictate that if we lack energy, the best way to have more is to use less. When you come home from work, sit in the recliner and save your energy. On Saturdays, save your energy by putting off mowing the yard or washing the car. But we know that the human body doesn't work that way. The more we exercise and use our energy, the more energy our bodies will produce.

That is also true of the Christian life. We are told to expel the energy of prayer, and we will have answered prayer (I John 5:14, 15). We are told to expel the energy of compassion and witnessing, and the result will be that we have more (Psalm 126:6). We are told to give materially for the right reasons, and God will bless us materially. (Matthew 7:11). These are biblical principles of how God blesses us conditionally.

Take Philippians 4:19:

> "But my God shall supply all your need according to His riches in glory by Christ Jesus."

It is, in context, a promise to those who have supplied the needs of missionaries by financial support. Because some have expelled the energy of giving, God will, in return, give to them so their needs will be met.

The same principle is collectively true of a church. Yes, there are tremendous pressures on churches these days. There are needs to be met, expectations to be fulfilled, and responsibilities to be carried out. The natural tendency is to think, "We should do something (or we should do more) for missions. But things are just so tight right now. The budget won't allow us to do anything at this time. We are right in the middle of a building program, and we can't afford it." It sounds so logical and practical. But there is a major problem: it does not take God into consideration. God will finance His work. Only one question must be answered: "Is the evangelization of the unreached the will of God?" The answer is a clear and resounding, "Yes!" Therefore, the only thing left for us to do is to obey God and leave the consequences to Him.

A church that places more of its focus and resources on missions is a church that will become more soul-conscious, not only for the lost and dying on the other side of the world, but also for the lost and dying on the other side of the block.

MISCONCEPTION NUMBER 9:

"Missions is a ministry of the church."

The reader might be asking, "How, in light of all that the Bible says and all you have written so far in this book, can you say the idea that 'missions is a ministry of the church' is a misconception?

Missions is not a ministry of the church; missions is the ministry of the church. Too many churches put their missions program under a convenient little committee, in a convenient little room, with a convenient little schedule. It becomes just one of many programs they take out and dust off periodically, re-evaluating and then re-shelving.

Friends, the very purpose of the church is missions! The very heartbeat of God, the responsibility of His people, and the cry of the unsaved is missions. Jesus does not leave us to debate, ponder, or pray for revelation as to what His purpose for His church is. He tells us in Matthew 28:19, 20,

"Go ye therefore, and teach all nations, baptizing them in the name of the Father, and of the Son, and of the Holy Ghost: Teaching them to observe all things whatsoever I have commanded you: and lo, I am with you always, even unto the end of the world."

Jesus tells us in Mark 16:15,

"Go ye into all the world, and preach the gospel to every creature."

He tells us in Acts 1:8,

"But ye shall receive power, after that the Holy Ghost is come upon you: and ye shall be witnesses unto me both in Jerusalem,

and in all Judea, and into Samaria, and unto the uttermost part of the earth."

The problem with many churches is they don't understand that it is God's church and God's plan. We are not given the option of coming up with our own agenda. Once we understand and accept His purpose, we can be a people of purpose. That purpose is to reach and teach the world about Jesus Christ. Everything else is part of the process.

MISCONCEPTION NUMBER 10:

"You ought to give to missions or be a missionary for the following reasons:"

1."You have so much, and they have so little."

This little motivational presentation goes something like, "Shame on you. You are going to leave church today and go out to a nice restaurant and eat while your brothers and sisters halfway around the world are going hungry. Shame on you! You come into a beautiful church building that's heated in the winter and cooled in the summer and sit in plush pews while the native church sits on the floor of a hot dung hut half a world away. You have health insurance so that you can go to the doctor any time you need while our countrymen can't even afford basic medical attentions. Shame on you!"

While there is plenty of truth in the fact that we have so much and the native church has so little, it is wrong to mistake that as an indication of our greed or indifference. All that we have is from God. God has blessed us and wonderfully met our needs, and we need not be ashamed at His blessings. Our shame, if there is any, could be in how little of God's blessings we have been willing to share with others.

You give because you love God and His people. I like the American custom of buying gifts for loved ones on Christmas, Valentine's Day, and anniversaries. Usually, this is not out of pressure or guilt, but out of the desire to show the other person how much we love them.

Our desire for missions should not be born out of guilt because the quality of life a person either suffers or enjoys. That is based on material items and temporary circumstances that pass away. We should reach out to our fellow man because we are concerned with his immortal soul.

2. "No one should hear the Gospel twice until everyone has heard it once."

While this statement sounds right, it really isn't. It is true that there is a great disparity in our world. Many in the West and in Europe have tremendous access to churches, preaching, and the truth of Jesus Christ, while those on the 10/40 window do not.

But does that really mean we should forget about the person who has heard the Gospel once and not accepted, just to reach out to the next one? How many times did God have to present His truth to us before we accepted it? For many, it was more than once. What is true is that we should preach the Gospel to every man, woman, and child that God brings before us, regardless of how many times he has heard it or where he lives.

3. "If God hasn't called you to stay in America, then He has called you to go."

This too is a well-meaning but erroneous missionary statement. God does have a plan for each of our lives and His plan requires some to go and some to stay. As we saw before, there are the goers and the senders. Romans 10:15 asks the question,

Taking the Gospel to the neediest and remotest regions...

Native church planters distributing the living word of God.

"THE WORD OF GOD SPEAKS"

GIVING WINGS TO NATIVE CHURCH PLANTERS
BY PROVIDING A MOTORBIKE OR BICYCLE

Providing Education and Help to Needy children...

We Support Schools and Children's Home Across Asia!

Our goal as a ministry is to give children the chance to hear about the God who created them, and loves them so much that He gave His life for them.

Jesus said, "Allow the little children to come to Me, and do not forbid them..."

Alpha Ministries reaches children through VBS and Children's Bible Clubs, where the children also enjoy a great time of fun and adventure.

Children participating in glass painting...

Alpha Medical Missions.....

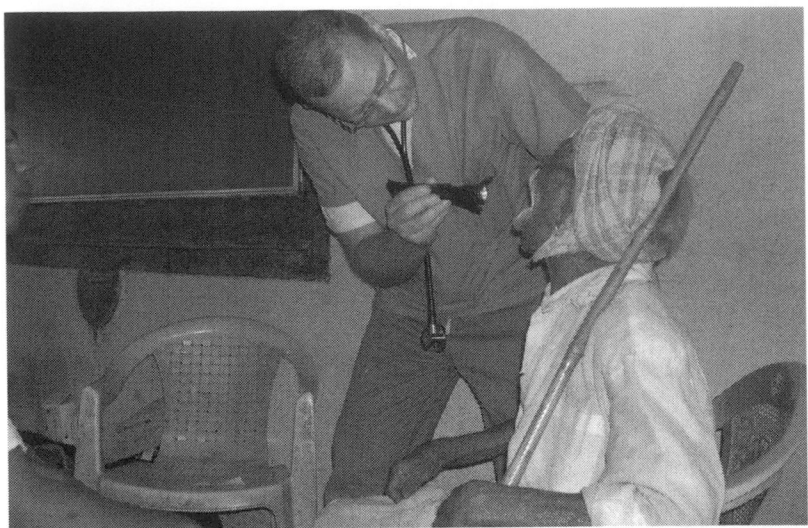

Alpha Medical Missions provide basic healthcare where there is limited or no access, treating simple conditions, which in a third world country can become debilitating without attention

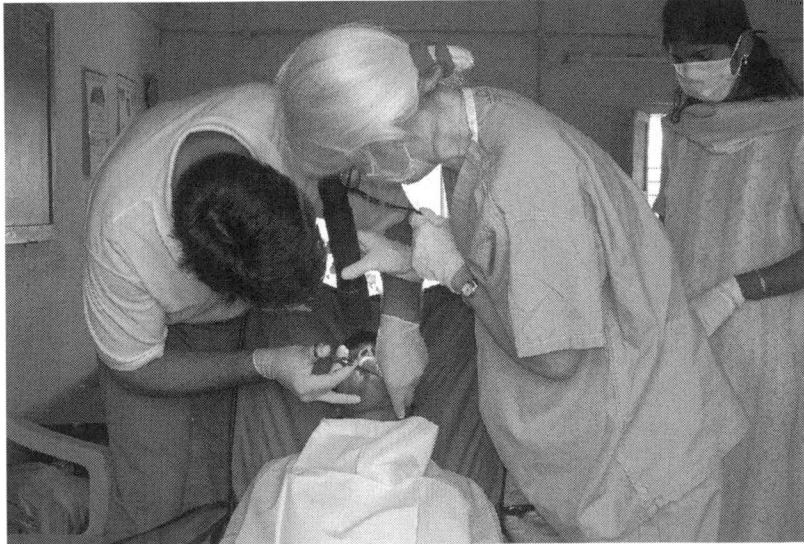

In addition, Alpha Medical Missions offer a testimony of Christ's compassion and a window of opportunity to reach the unreached.

Living water project...

"...give a cup of water to drink in my name, because ye belong to Christ..." (Mark 9:41)

"How shall they [these are the goers] preach except they be sent [these are the senders]…."

In light of this idea, one may ask, "Which group is more important, and which group is in God's will, the goers or the senders?" The answer is neither and both. The important question is this: What has God called you to do? If He has called you to go, then go. If He has called you to send others, then send others.

The interesting thing about the scope of our responsibility as seen in Acts 1:8 is that while we minister as senders to the regions beyond in Jerusalem, we are actually goers to our own Jerusalem. Once goers get to where God has sent them to go, they become goers and senders. They are always taking the message of Christ to their own neighborhood personally (goers) and helping to take that message to those beyond their reach (senders).

4. "God is finished with North American missionaries."

Nothing could be further from the truth. My colleague and missionary Dr. Dan Reichard, who helped me put this book together, was saved at the age of 22 while he was an airman in the United States Air Force. He was led to Christ through the missionary ministry to the servicemen right here in America. Thank God for North American men and women who are faithfully serving on missions fields around the world, including the United States!

If God has called you to go and you can enter and minister in that country, GO! Western missions and native missions are not opposites, nor are they rivals. They are each doing what God has called them to do in the place that God has called them to go. Other "Buts:"

"But their hearts are hardened by world religions. How can they be saved?"

"With man it is impossible; with God all things are possible."
(Matthew 19:26)

We openly admit that we do not do the saving. It is God who does the saving through the outward proclaiming of His Word and the inward prompting of His Holy Spirit. We are the "seed bearers." Psalm 126:6 says,

"He that goeth forth and weepeth, bearing precious seed, shall doubtless come again with rejoicing, bringing his sheaves with him."

The seed is the Word of God, the Bible. Paul declared that,

"Faith cometh by hearing, and hearing by the Word of God."
(Romans 10:17)

"But the countries where the unreached people groups live won't allow Christianity to be legalized."

"I exhort therefore, that, first of all, supplications, prayers, intercessions, and giving of thanks, be made for all men; For kings and for all that are in authority; that we may lead a quiet and peaceable life in all godliness and honesty." (I Timothy 2:1, 2)

The Gospel is too powerful, the power of God is too strong, and the passion of His children too great to be stopped by man-made barriers. When faced with the choice to avoid further persecution by no longer preaching Christ or to suffer for the cause of Christ,

"Peter and John answered and said (unto them), 'Whether it be

right in the sight of God to hearken unto you more than unto God, judge ye. For we cannot but speak the things which we have seen and heard."' (Acts 4:19, 20)

"But they won't accept Christ."

In the context of prayer, Paul goes on to says,

"...in the sight of God our Savior; who will have all men to be saved and to come unto the knowledge of the truth."
(I Timothy 2:3b, 4)

God is omnipotent. People will accept Christ. They are accepting Christ at the rate of one and a half million new believers each day. A fire is burning among the dry kindling of the hearts and souls that have for too long been denied the life-giving Living Water that will quench the hearts of men and women. Politicians have tried to denounce Him. Lawmakers have tried to forbid him. Religious "false prophets" have tried to explain Him away, and yet He continues undaunted on His quest of saving and redeeming mankind from the emptiness and loneliness of their lost-ness.

Very often, churches will give out a prayer list during the mid-week prayer service. It will have a list of the praises and the prayer requests that had been called in during the week. One of my friends remembered a moment years ago, the first time someone wrote in the prayer request, "Pray for the fall of communism in the Soviet Union."

He said, "I am sure I smirked (if not outwardly, then at least on the inside) when I read that. I thought, 'God isn't going to take away communism from the Soviet Union.' I could even make a fairly good argument from eschatology as to why this wouldn't happen. Week after week, month after month, year after year, this same person would call in this same prayer request, and I am sure that if I ever did actually pray for the 'fall of communism' it was half-hearted at best…but someone was praying."

Think of the Berlin Wall, the symbol of communist power and authority in Europe and the Soviet Union, being taken down by sledgehammers and the hands of peasants and politicians alike. What did the destruction of the wall mean? It meant that communism had fallen in the Soviet Union. It meant that the Soviet Union had ceased to exist.

Was it because the Soviet Union crumbled amidst the university student freedom movement? Was it because of a failing economy? No! God did it, and God did it because people prayed. And by the way, God didn't do it so that Coca Cola could open up the Eastern Europe soft drink market. God didn't do it so that Levi jeans could finally be sold on the open market. God did it so that the millions of people who had been held in darkness and chains of that godless, atheistic empire could finally behold the glorious light of the Gospel of Jesus Christ.

"But they are too steeped in their own false religions to turn to Christ."

Listen to what William Carey, pioneer missionary to India, said: "He, who raised the Scottish and brutalized Britons to sit in heavenly places in Christ Jesus, can raise these slaves of superstition, purify their hearts by faith, and make them worshippers of the one God in spirit and truth. He will banish all the gods of India and cause these very idolaters to cast their idols to the moles and to the bats, and renounce forever the work of their own hands."

If God can save you and me, stubborn sinners who love their sin, He can surely save anyone. God can do that and God is doing that.

"Among many who sought to deter me, was one dear old
Christian gentleman, whose crowning argument always was,
"The cannibals! You will be eaten by cannibals!"
At last I replied, "Mr. Dickson, you are advanced in years now,
and your own prospect is soon to be laid in the grave, there to be
eaten by worms; I confess to you, that if I can
but live and die serving and honouring the Lord Jesus,
it will make no difference to me whether I am eaten
by cannibals or by worms."

-John G. Paton

"Stop telling God how big your mountain is!
Instead, tell your mountain how big your God is"

- Dr. Jerry Falwell Sr.,
Founder Liberty University

Our goal as a ministry is to train and send out natives to the unreached areas where Christ is not preached.

As we look to the future our mission is to train 100,000 church planters in Asia and, to plant 100,000 churches where no church exists.

Join in the Passage

Chapter 7

> *"The command has been to "go," but we have stayed - in body, gifts, prayer and influence. He has asked us to be witnesses unto the uttermost parts of the earth . . . But 99 percent of Christians have kept puttering around in the homeland."*
> *- Robert Savage*

Someone asked Vince Lombardi, arguably the greatest football coach in history, "Coach, what is the definition of football?" Lombardi thought for a few moments and responded, "Football is the act of 22 men on the field who are desperately in the need of rest, being watched by 45,000 men in the stands desperately in the need of exercise."

It was a good answer and one that is appropriate for many Christians. Too often, we sit in the pews and let the "professionals" do the work. We sit on our wallets and let the "givers" do the giving. We ignore the needs of those around us and let the "prayer warriors" do the interceding. We fail to heed the cries of the lost and let the "missionaries" do the witnessing. We invite you to get up and leave the stands. Get out on the field and be a participant in the Passage to the Unreached. Don't just be saved and satisfied. Let us speed up the mission of the church and finish the task so that God can fill the whole earth with His Glory. We shall see Him face to face and become like Him (1 John 3:2). This is our vision and this is our prayer as we anticipate His coming for our glorification.

One of the most effective approaches to the Passage you can take is partnering with the native church. Every time I hear the story of a miracle that has occurred or a family that has been saved from idolatry through a native missions worker, I cannot help but pair, in my mind, the family in America that made it all possible.

Native missionaries are on the front lines, but just like David's troops, they need support from behind. They are not asking for reinforcements so they can evacuate out of harm's way. All they are asking for is the ammunition to pierce the hearts and minds of the lost entrenched in front of them. They are asking for Bibles. They are asking for our prayers. They are asking for the funds to plant churches, develop godly leaders, distribute medicine, provide clean water, and so much more.

These men and women have been called by God to do what we cannot. Our tongues find it difficult to learn and speak the languages. The extreme distances make it hard for us to travel and engage. But, by the grace of God and the power of the body of Christ working in unison, the native missionary's legs can peddle a bicycle to the most remote regions. His words flow effortlessly when he speaks about God and His limitless love.

Have you been called by God to provide the encouragement, the confidence, and the support to the front lines? God has not called us to support everyone in the world. But He has called us to support those He puts before us. Supporting these pastors and their families encourages them to know that they are not alone. It gives them one more reason to sing about God who loves and provides for them.

It is our opportunity to take something very little and give it eternal significance. It creates an opportunity for a lost soul to know the love of God, as told to them from someone freed from idolatrous bondage. It plants a tree of life that branches to their children, their grandchildren, their great-grandchildren, and generations beyond.

Jesus said, "Pray ye therefore the Lord of the harvest, that he will send forth laborers into his harvest." That is the answer to the need. If we pray, God will send. If we send, men will hear. If men hear, some will believe. It all begins by a fervent commitment to pray. Pray as if the eternal destiny of mankind is at stake…because it is.

Alpha Ministries is dedicated to reaching the unreached. We invite you to join us in this great endeavor. Please go to alphaministries.net to learn how you can be part of our different projects ranging from Bible distribution and church planting, to medical missions and child sponsorship.

Alpha Ministries has been planting churches for over five decades in one of the most strategic mission fields in the world – the 10/40 Window. Since our founding in South Asia, Alpha Ministries has been training and mobilizing native missionaries through a dynamic learning process. Individuals trained through this program are sent out with a renewed vision for pioneer church planting.

Appendix:
The Model Church

What model would we use if we were presenting a model missionary church? Certainly we could point out a number of historical and contemporary churches that have made a significant contribution to missions. We might call any number of them the model church. But, in reality, any model church or missionary program is only going to be successful if it is modeled after biblical principles. So let's cut out the middleman. Let's go directly to the Scriptures to look at our "model church and missionary example."

Perhaps the church of Jerusalem is the model church. After all:

1. The church of Jerusalem was the church that the Holy Spirit met with in the upper room.
2. The church of Jerusalem was the church that the Apostles themselves led in the early days of church history.
3. The church of Jerusalem was a church that was marked by mighty preaching and teaching.
4. The church of Jerusalem was a church that was marked by great generosity and evangelistic fervor.
5. The church of Jerusalem was a church that experienced tremendous spiritual and numeric growth.

Yet, the church of Jerusalem is not the church that we will designate as the "model church." After all, it was that Jerusalem church that Christ Himself gave the command of Acts 1:8, to witness Christ in Jerusalem, Judea, Samaria, and to the uttermost parts of the earth. While the Word of God was flowing through the streets of Jerusalem, there was still a drought of gospel preaching just beyond the walls of that great city. It is not until Acts 8:1 that we see the disciples of the Jerusalem church comply with the command of Acts 1:8. And even then it was not necessarily motivated by a burden to obey the Great Commission. It is not motivated by a broken-hearted people who are leaving their jobs, homes, families, and securities to take the good news of the Gospel to those who had not heard. It was motivated by God's instrument of persecution.

Acts 8:1 gives the account of this missionary thrust:

"And Saul was consenting unto his death [Stephen's, the first martyr of the church]. And at that time there was a great persecution against the church which was at Jerusalem; and they were all scattered abroad throughout the regions of Judea and Samaria, except the apostles."

Isn't it tragic to realize that the disciples didn't obey the command of Acts 1:8 until they feared for their lives? Did you notice where they went? They went into the regions of Judea and Samaria. Amazing isn't it? That's where God wanted them to go all along. The bottom line is that a church can have a great beginning, great personnel, and a great program but still miss out on that which is at the very center of God's heart. Jerusalem did it. In Revelation 2:4 the church of Ephesus did it. It can happen to them, and it can happen to us. Perhaps it already has.

Then what is the model church in regard to missions? It is the church of Antioch. In reality, many of you reading this will say, "I didn't even know that there was a church at Antioch." After all, we are somewhat familiar with the churches that the New Testament writers addressed in specific epistles, such as the church at Rome, the church at Corinth, the church at Galatia, the church at Ephesus, the church at Philippi, the church at Colossi, and the church at Thessalonica. But the church of Antioch?

The church of Antioch is the very model church in regards to missions. Note the following texts in Acts 13:1-3 and Acts 14:26-28:

"Now there were in the church that was at Antioch certain prophets and teachers; as Barnabas and Simeon that is called Niger, and Lucius of Cyrene and Manaen, which had been brought up with Herod the tetrarch, and Saul. As they ministered to the Lord and fasted, the Holy Ghost said, Separate me Barnabas and Saul for the work whereunto I have called thee, And when they had fasted and prayed and laid their hands on them, they sent them away." Acts 13:1-3.

And, after their first missionary journey, Acts 14:26-28, says,

"And thence sailed to Antioch from whence they had been recommended to the grace of God for the work which they fulfilled. And when they were come, and had gathered the church [at Antioch] together, they rehearsed all that God had done with them, and how He had opened the door of faith unto the Gentiles. And there they abode long time with the disciples."

Here are some of the qualities that make the church of Antioch the "model missionary church:"

1. They were a church that was already busy serving God. In Acts 13:2, it is said that they "ministered to the Lord." This doesn't mean that the believers in the church at Jerusalem didn't minister to the Lord. Neither does it mean that God blesses a busy church. If most of our churches are anything, they are busy. We have more than enough programs, committees, meetings, schedules, and activities. It is a testimony to the church at Antioch that they were already busy before the Holy Spirit gave them the "go ahead" on the next phase of their task. Did you ever notice in the Bible that God always calls busy people? He doesn't call lazy people to do His work. This church was already

busy doing everything that the church at Jerusalem was doing.

2. They had discovered the key to hearing God speak. In Acts 13:2, 3, the Bible says that while they ministered to the Lord, they prayed and fasted. As they did these three things, God opened a door for them. Someone once said, "Beware of the barrenness of business." While it is true that the church at Antioch was a busy church, they were busy because they heard God speak, and did what He told them to do. Perhaps we need to spend more time listening to God.

3. They were a church of vision. Jesus had told His disciples in John 4:35b,

"...lift up your eyes, and look on the fields; for they are white already to harvest."

Notice that Jesus had to teach His disciples that they must, in order to see things from God's perspective, first lift up their eyes. It is a natural tendency of man to look at his own needs and wants and not the needs of others. Jesus is saying that we must see the world through His eyes. That is what vision is all about. The Antioch church saw the world the way that Jesus saw it. Their vision was God's vision, and God's vision was their vision. Can we truly say that?

4. They were a church that made God's priorities their priorities. A story is told of the commander of a British troop in Trenton, New Jersey during the Revolutionary War. The commander was warned through a note that George Washington was crossing the Delaware River. He was rather preoccupied by a card game and put the slip into his pocket and finished the game. When the game was over, he pulled the piece of paper out of his pocket and was shocked to read its content. Washington had already made his way across. As a result, the commander lost his life and 50 percent of his troops were killed. The remaining troops

were taken prisoners. They had not responded to the call with urgency. But, the church at Antioch had a sense of urgency. We can see that from the following examples:

a. They did what they did because God said to. The greatest reason to do something is simply because God said to. Every parent has said, or has been tempted to say to his child, "Because I said so." Now, we are not advocating that we shouldn't carefully explain the rules and expectations to our children, but after the explanation comes obedience. Christ had already explained the Great Commission and His plan for world evangelism to His disciples. He had already explained it to Jerusalem as well. Now it was time to, as a famous sneaker ad says, "Just do it." The church of Antioch, "Just did it."

b. They gave the "best and the brightest" for missions. In some of the overseas cultures we have lived, there is a tendency sometimes, even for good and sincere Christian parents, to discourage the brightest of their children from the ministry. We are aware of many who have resisted the calling of their best children into the ministry while encouraging the "least talented" or the "least gifted" to go into the ministry. The bottom line for this practice is that, in cultures without retirement insurance, social security, etc., the parents depend on their working children to support them in their old age. The better the child's job and the more it pays, then the better standard of living and the more financial security the parent has.

c. Antioch didn't discourage their brightest and their best. They didn't think about themselves, what they considered best for them, or if the sacrifice was too great. They sent several of the godliest and most prominent members of their church as foreign missionaries. In reality, the Holy Spirit had already told them whom to send. Their choice was not whom to send but whether or not to obey God. They obeyed God with joy and thanksgiving. Jesus said, "Pray ye the Lord of the harvest that

He will send forth laborers into his harvest." Are we? Are we willing to ask God to call our children into fulltime, vocational ministry even though it might be dangerous? Even though it will likely take them away from us? Even though it will likely pay far less than they could make if they pursued other vocational options? This is ultimately a test of obedience. We love God enough to pray that He will call forth laborers into the harvest, but do we love Him and trust Him enough to pray that He will call our children to the work? Thank God Antioch did.

5. They were a courageous church.

• **It took courage to leave the comparatively safe confines of the Antioch fellowship and go to the "regions beyond."**

A "mission's trip" was unheard of in those days. But God said to "separate" them for the "work whereunto I have called them." The people of Antioch didn't know what that work was. They didn't know where that work would take them. They didn't know how long that work would cause them to be gone. They didn't know what the personal cost of that "separation" would be. But they did know the God who called them to do it, and they knew that they could trust Him.

Imagine what it was like to travel in those days. They didn't have trains, airplanes, or comfortable cars. When we travel in North India, we use all available means of transportation. Often the roads are bad, the cars are hot, the journey is long, the accommodations are lacking, and the trip is exhausting. But the worst day of travel today is better than the best day of travel for Paul and Barnabas. Travel was always difficult, and it was almost always dangerous. They were basically given a one-way ticket to who knows where. Why did they go? Because they knew that the one who was sending them knew where they were going. They knew that He would be there with them every step of the way. And that was enough for them.

- **It took courage to step out and do what no other church had done before.** Sometimes, as adults, we criticize teenagers for "caving in" to peer pressure. Admit it. We adults are just as conscious about what others are going to think. The church of Antioch determined that obedience is the right thing to do even if no one else is doing it. We know of many good churches that are excited about what God is doing through Alpha Ministries in the area of reaching the unreached people groups of Asia. Yet, when they share their enthusiasm with other churches or church leaders within their fellowships or denominations, they are often discouraged by the voices of "but we've never done it that way before" or "but it doesn't fit into our twenty year plan" or "just hang on for a while, we have something in the works for Asia." Thank God for the Antioch church. They realized that obedience is not a democracy nor is it an issue to be voted on. They simply did what God called them to do.

- **It was a church that understood the source of its power.** The church of Antioch didn't just "welcome" the Holy Spirit into its midst for a brief business meeting to discuss missions. They understood that it was the Holy Spirit who could give strength for the labor, wisdom for the details, provision for the journey, and protection from the dangers. It was the Holy Spirit who would change the lives of those reached by the glorious Gospel of Christ. This same Paul, in speaking of the Gospel, will later say,

"For I am not ashamed of the Gospel of Christ; for it is the power of God unto salvation to everyone that believeth; to the Jew first, and also to the Greek [Gentile]" Romans 1:16 .

Have you ever noticed that God already knew that the mission of world evangelization was so enormous and so overwhelming that we couldn't do it in our own power or strength? Right before two separate and key "Great Commissions," Jesus placed a strategic promise that His power would go before us in this undertaking. In the often quoted Matthew 28:19, 20 Great Commission, Jesus begins by first promising His disciples,

> *"All power is given unto me in heaven and in earth (Matt. 28: 18b) . . . Go ye therefore...."*

A simple rule of hermeneutics reminds us, "Whenever you find the word *therefore*, read back a few verses and see what it is there for." In other words, the "therefore" of Christ's power is "there for" the purpose of fulfilling the command for worldwide evangelism. Again, in Acts 1:8a, Jesus said,

> "But ye shall receive power, after that the Holy Ghost is come upon you: and ye shall be witnesses unto me . . ."

D.L. Moody, speaking on whether or not the Gospel needs defending, said, "The Gospel does not need to be defended. It is like a roaring lion that needs not be defended but simply released."

• It was a church that "practiced what they preached." Have you ever watched a show about sharks? It usually goes something like this: A scientist, safely nestled in the security of a shark cage, watches and observes sharks from a distance. Now, there is nothing wrong with that. That's the way shark watching should be done.

But, when it comes to missions, that's not the way to be an "Antioch church." I have a friend who traveled with several nationally known church growth ministries. He told me that it was a joy to meet many pastors and church leaders from around the country. Many would travel great distances and spend valuable time and resources to attend these seminars in order to learn how to be a "spiritually healthy church." He said that in time he "began to realize that some who attend such conferences aren't really looking for something that will really cause their membership to grow spiritually and thus numerically. They want a new idea or a new 'gimmick.' They want a 'canned' program which they can delegate to someone else to implement that would result in the church's growing numerically, financially, and in reputation among their neighboring churches." Biblical church growth is not that. Alpha Ministries is not that either. The Antioch church wasn't that, and you can be sure that God is not!

Perhaps you have heard this familiar missions illustration about a local fire station. It seems that a visitor came to a local fire station to see what firemen did. He found one fireman polishing the pole that allowed the firemen to slide down from their sleeping quarters to the area where the fire trucks were parked. When asked what his job was, he replied, "My job is to polish the pole." Another fireman was busy straightening the hoses. When asked what his job was, he replied, "My job is to straighten out the hoses." A third fireman was washing the fire truck. When asked what his job was, he replied, "My job is to wash the fire truck." About that time, the alarm sounded and the radio broadcast the news that a nearby building was on fire. Seemingly innocuous to the alarm were the three firemen. One continued to polish the pole, one continued to straighten the hoses, and one continued to wash the truck. The visitor frantically shouted to the firemen that a building was on fire and that they should leave immediately to put the fire out and rescue the people who might be inside. The one fireman replied, "My job is to make sure that this pole is shiny." Another said, "My job is to make sure the hoses are straight." The last, still washing the truck, said, "My job is to make sure that the truck is clean." Alas, the house burned, and no one inside escaped.

The obvious moral is that the firemen had been doing their specific tasks for so long that they had forgotten that their tasks were simply a means to an end of accomplishing a greater task: to put out fires and save lives. Too often, when confronted with the cries of a lost and dying world desperately in need of Jesus Christ, we as a church reply, "That's not my job. My job is to sing in the choir. My job is to serve on a committee. My job is to teach a Sunday school class, and so on." We fail to realize that the ultimate goal of all that we do is to fulfill our God-given, Christ-commissioned responsibility, the Great Commission.

The church of Antioch resisted the temptation to spend time simply talking about world evangelism. They resisted the tendency to debate the issues, organize committees, and devise feasibility studies to examine every aspect of the issue. Don't get me wrong. We need to plan and we need to prepare. But at some point, we need to launch out by faith and do something for the glory of God. If all of our planning and all of our examining and all of our talking do not cause us to step out and, as William Carey said, "Expect great things from God and attempt great things for God," then we are just playing church. We are just going through the motions if we are not "attempting great things for God." In other words, the pole is polished. The hoses are straight. The truck is washed. Yet multitudes slip out into eternity each day, unwarned, untold, lost!

So now we have a model church. Antioch did something that impacted their world for Christ. They left behind a legacy that still bears fruit and a model that is still worthy of emulating.

ABOUT AUTHORS...

Brother Bennie is the Executive Vice President of Alpha Ministries and serves as the President of Leadership Development, at ALPHA IMPACT LEADERSHIP SEMINARS (Passion for God and people... Equip church leaders and planters.) Their objective is to train 100,000 leaders to plant 100,000 churches where no church exists.

Brother Bennie followed in the footsteps of his parents who are church planting missionaries in Northern India. In 1994, he resigned his job in the medical field in New York City to be involved in the work of Alpha Ministries. He later received an invitation from Dr. Jerry Falwell to join Liberty Bible Institute. A series of life changing experiences happened there under the leadership of Dr. Harold L. Willmington.

Brother Bennie spends a majority of his time in South Asian countries and Africa, organizing and speaking in seminars and leadership training. He is called to motivate, mobilize, and support the national evangelists and pastors to reach the least-reached for Jesus Christ. Whether it is mentoring and serving in his local church or on the mission field, God has blessed and empowered him with the ability to encourage others and to nurture the belief in God's endless possibilities.

His purpose statement: To make Christ known in places where they have never heard the Gospel, mobilizing natives to accomplish God's global agenda among the least-reached. Brother Bennie and Lina were married in 1990. They have three children; Faith-Hannah, Ben-Israel and Joy-Ruth. They live near Lynchburg, Virginia.

Dan Reichard grew up disoriented from God, joined the Air Force, was shown Christ by fellow servicemen, and was led to a commitment by a missionary to the military. While in the U.S. Air Force he was called to ministry.

He married Shelley, his childhood sweetheart. He did his B.A. in Biblical Studies from Tennessee Temple University, and his Masters in Education from Temple Baptist Theological Seminary. Dan, Shelley, and their three children went to the Philippines as missionaries with the Association of Baptists for World Evangelism. They returned to the states where Dan pastored several churches, earned a Th.D. from Trinity Theological Seminary, became a writer and speaker for Church Growth Institute and Ephesians 4 Ministries, and served 16 years as principal of a Christian school.

In 1998 he was speaking to 750 native missionaries at Alpha Ministries' national IMPACT leadership conference in North India when Hindu militants broke into the meeting and severely beat many of them. The experience changed Dan's life, and in 2006 he became Missionary-at-Large with Advancing Native Missions. He also is V.P. for Spiritual Affairs, directs the Far East Desk, and heads its Operation Barnabas International program that offers seminars of encouragement to groups of native missionaries.

BIBLIOGRAPHY

1. "Praying Through the Window," last modified October 1999, http://www.ad2000.org/1040ovr.htm

2. "Records of the 1983 International Conference for Itinerant Evangelists (Amsterdam 83) - Collection 253," last modified 2005, http://www.wheaton.edu/bgc/archives/GUIDES/253.htm

3. "A Tribute to Dr. Bill Bright - Founder of Campus Crusade for Christ," last accessed August 2011, http://retirementwithapurpose.com/growth/kjktributebb.html

4. "10/40 Window: Do you need to be stirred to action?" last modified June 2011, http://home.snu.edu/~HCULBERT/1040.htm

5. "Amsterdam 2000 Called the Most Multinational Event Ever" last modified, July 2000, http://www.christianitytoday.com/ct/2000/julyweb-only/32.0d.html

6. Bush, Louis and Beverly Pegues. The Move of the Holy Spirit in the 10/40 Window. Seattle: Ywam Publishing, 1999.

7. Samuel, Vinay and Chris Sugden. Mission as Transformation: A Theology of the Whole Gospel. Oxford: Regnum, 1999.

8. Blaikie, William Garden. The Personal Life of David Livingstone. (New York: Fleming H. Revell Company, 1881) Accessed August 2011, http://books.google.com/books?id=gRm-wMEPRO8C

9. "Bill Bright, 1921-2003", accessed August 2001, http://billbright.ccci.org/public/

The publisher has made every effort to trace the ownership of all quotations and to request appropriate permissions. In the event of a question arising from the use of a quotation, we regret any error made and will be pleased to make the necessary correction in future edition of this book.

A BIBLE FOR EVERY BACKPACK

The author's proceeds from this book will benefit project
"A Bible in a Backpack"

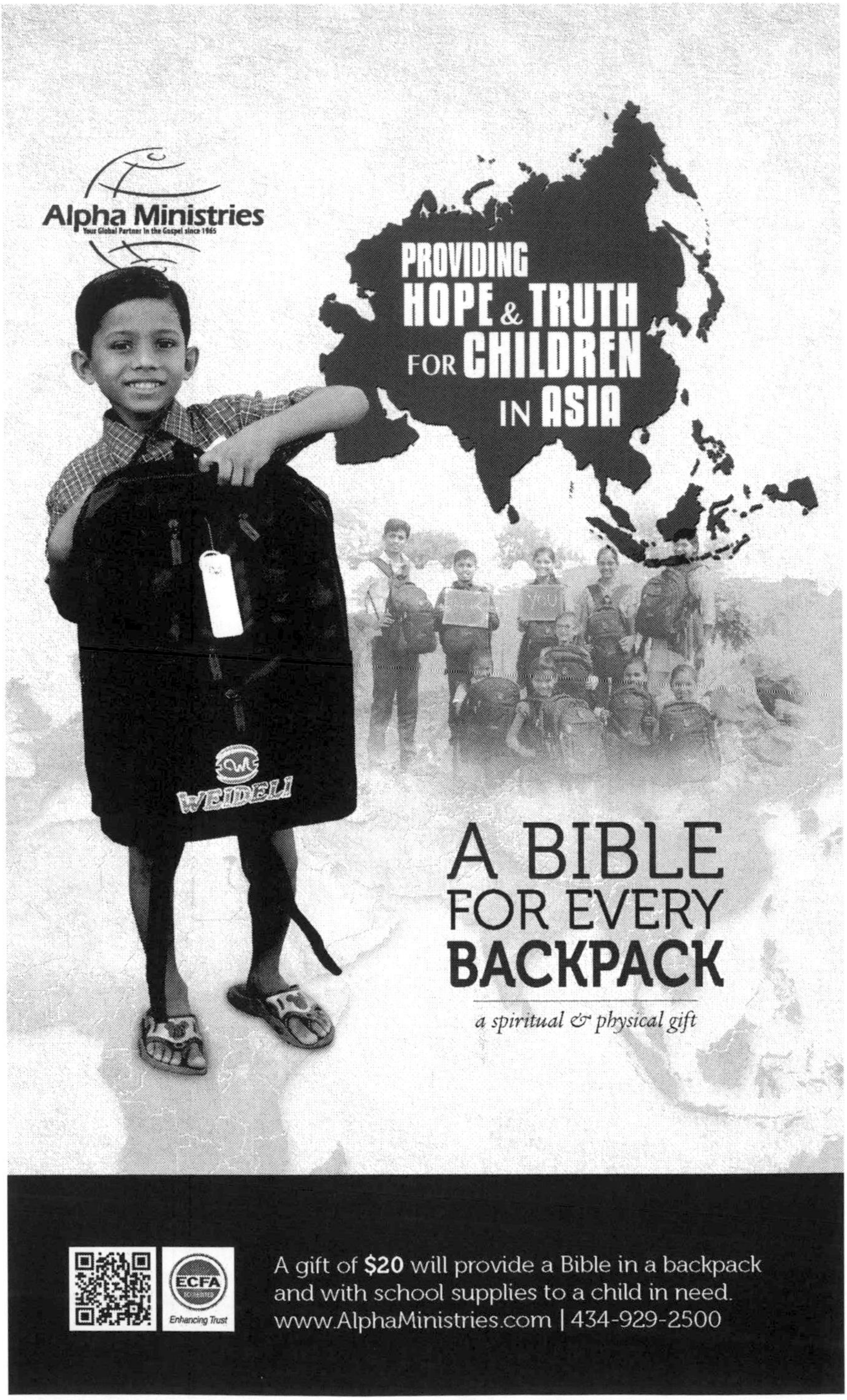
Alpha Ministries
Your Global Partner in the Gospel since 1965
PROVIDING HOPE & TRUTH FOR CHILDREN IN ASIA
WEIDELI
A BIBLE FOR EVERY BACKPACK
a spiritual & physical gift
ECFA
Enhancing Trust
A gift of $20 will provide a Bible in a backpack and with school supplies to a child in need.
www.AlphaMinistries.com | 434-929-2500

The Need

All children face similar struggles, but those in impoverished countries have compounded problems due to the extremely difficult daily circumstances. Schooling is critical but for many poor children, their families cannot afford even the simple school supplies they need.

The Solution

Alpha Ministries places a Bible in a backpack filled with grade-specific supplies (notebooks, pencils, pens, erasers, sharpeners, and more). The school supplies help children succeed in their education, while the Bible gives them the very Word of God, lasting Truth planted in their hearts!

The Impact

Since 2004, Alpha Ministries has distributed nearly 15,000 Bibles in a Backpack. The Bible in a Backpack communicates hope and truth to young people.

The Cost

For a gift of $20 you can provide a Bible in a Backpack for a needy child.

Yes! I want to offer hope and truth of Christ to children to Asia!

Here is my gift of $_____ to provide_____ for a needy child in Asia!

☐ $20 to provide a Backpack, Bible & School supplies.
☐ $10 to provide school supplies to a child striving to get a quality education.
☐ $6 to provide a new backpack to a child who would not otherwise have one.
☐ $4 to place a Bible in the hand of a child.

Name _____

Address_____

City_____State_____Zip_____

Phone_____ Email__ _____

To ensure financial accountability Alpha Ministries is a member of the Evangelical Council for Financial Accountability (ECFA). Alpha Ministries is a 501(c)(3) nonprofit charitable organization. All donations to Alpha Ministries are income tax deductible to the extent allowed by law. Make all checks payable to Alpha Ministries. To give online visit www.AlphaMinistries.com

Pray For

BROTHER BENNIE & LINA

WHERE THERE IS DARKNESS, WE BRING THE LIGHT OF CHRIST!
Population of India: 1.5 Billion
Religion: **74.3%** Hindus   **14.2%** Muslims   **5.8%** Christians
(2,533 people groups of which 2,229 are unreached by the Gospel)

Alpha Ministries

Phone: **434.546.3069** Email: **benny@alphaministries.com**

PRAY

"We can scarcely be too lavish in our attention to the improvement of our native brethren. It is only by means of native preachers that we can hope for the universal spread of the Gospel throughout this immense continent." – **William Carey**

William Carey was the "Father of Modern Missions" and a pioneer missionary to India. He understood the value of equipping native believers to effectively reach the lost of their own culture and home. A native missionary and church planter is a believer who has committed his or her life to reach his or her own people with the Gospel of Jesus Christ, no matter the difficulty or cost.

BECOME A MVP PARTNER

(Most Valuable Prayer-Partner)

"...The effectual fervent prayer of a righteous man availeth much." James 5:16b

Join our MVP Partners Team – prayer was the first instruction Christ gave regarding making disciples and we take that very seriously. Become an MVP Partner by Joining Our Mission Valuable Prayer-Partners

"Therefore pray the Lord of the harvest to send out laborers into His harvest." Matthew 9:38.

It is His harvest and God is sending out His faithful workers. By making a monthly commitment to praying, you will be creating a lasting difference in the lives of children and families in some of the poorest regions in the world. We know in complete confidence that prayer is the most powerful way in which you can impact the world for God's kingdom and for believers ministering on the frontlines every you're your faithful prayer will act as a daily necessity and source of strength. We experience answered prayers so often that we frequently hear our frontline messengers say with confidence: "We prayed, so of course God will do it!"

We ask that you join our Missions Valuable Prayer-Partners and become a force of over 100,000 Alpha Missions friends around the world covering Pastor Mathews Cherian, the persecuted saints and Alpha Ministries in prayer. Thank you for being willing to be an MVP Partner. May the Lord bless you as you intercede in prayer!

Prayer brings powerful change beyond the limits of labor and funding. Watch as God authors and perfects our faith by being a part of answered prayer. Not everyone can give or go, but every believer can pray.

We invite you to pray for the multifaceted ministries of Alpha Ministries as well as our native church planters and staff continue laboring to reach the millions of unreached in Asia and West Africa. Your prayers for our ministry and the children we serve truly make an eternal difference.

"Prayer needs no passport, visa or work permit. There is no such thing as a 'closed

country' as far as prayer is concerned...much of the history of the mission could be written in terms of God moving in response to persistent prayer."
-**Stephan Gaukroger**

SEND AND PARTNER
PHILIPPIANS 1:5-6

Support a Frontline Messenger today! There are over 2.7 billion people on earth today who have never heard the name of Jesus Christ and are living enslaved to idols and pagan rituals that have no power to give everlasting hope or peace. 97% of these unreached people live in the 10/40 window which holds less than 1% of all Gospel literature and Christian broadcasting. Not only do the unreached in this region have little chance to hear about Jesus, but often battle serious consequences of poverty including the scarcity of clean water and the brutal caste system.

By financially supporting a native missionary, you'll be personally taking part in ministering to the lost men and women of some of the most unreached places on Earth. These local missionaries need support from Christians around the world to share the love of Christ with lost villages and entire people groups.

COMMIT TO GIVE
Philippians 4:15-17

If world evangelism is God's will, then invest your time and talents among those who need to be evangelized! Hundreds of dedicated Christians give sacrificially every year to support the church planters and the mission work of Alpha Ministries. They have the thrill of knowing that they are making an impact on the frontlines of advancing the Kingdom of God.

COMMIT TO GO
Acts 1:8

The challenges and opportunities in Asia and East & West Africa are enormous. Join other individuals from across the US to form ministry teams that will teach, reach, and serve through a short-term mission trip. This is a great way to catch a vision for the unreached firsthand and personally become the hands and feet of Christ.

Be a part of the work God has equipped you for by developing leadership skills within our ministry partners, teaching at seminars and National Conferences, and taking part on one of our various medical missions.

OUR FINANCIAL COMMITMENT

We at Alpha Ministries strive to be financially accountable to our donors and to the communities we serve. We recognize that the resources at our disposal are not our own and are a sacred trust from God through our donors. Therefore, we do everything we can to keep our overhead low in order to be good stewards with the funds entrusted to us.

We subscribe to a written statement of faith clearly affirming our commitment to the evangelical Christian doctrine. Advancing the gospel of Jesus Christ and Planting Churches Where no Church Exists is the objective of our financial conduct.

Alpha Ministries is a member of the **Evangelical Council of Financial Accountability**. We seek to conduct God's work with the highest standards of integrity. We obtain an annual audit by an independent public accounting firm with financial statements prepared in accordance with generally accepted accounting principles. We gladly provide copies of our current audited financial statements upon written request.

We are governed by a Board that meets twice a year. Our Board discusses major issues facing the ministry, oversees finances, establishes budgets and evaluates projects and accomplishments. Board members do not receive a salary or any other compensation.

We welcome your donation as God directs – no matter the amount. Thank you! Your generous gift improves lives and gives hope and help to advance the gospel. No gift is too small when combined with the power of many gifts.

Alpha Ministries is a 501(c)(3) organization, and all gifts are tax deductible to the full extent allowed by law.

NOTE TO THE READER

We invite you to share your response to the message of this book by writing to us. If you would like to help us, please write to us or send your gift to:

Alpha Ministries

P.O. Box 444,

Madison Heights, VA. 24572-0444

Call 1- 434-929-2500

Visit our website at www.AlphaMinistries.com

BACK COVER

36120609R00090

Made in the USA
Middletown, DE
15 February 2019